Social Security in the United Kingdom

Social Security in the United Kingdom

Contracting Out of the System

John C. Goodman

American Enterprise Institute for Public Policy Research
Washington and London

193043

John C. Goodman is assistant professor of economics and director of the Center for Health Policy Studies, University of Dallas.

The author thanks Clive Smee, senior economic adviser for the Department of Health and Social Security in London, and C. Mark Dadd, first secretary economics, British embassy, Washington, D.C., for helpful comments on this manuscript; Lawrence Streit for help in the preparation of the statistical tables; and Susan Tully, Bridgett Gaines, Sue Stevens, and Kate Hohlt for help in the preparation of the manuscript. The author also thanks Colin Campbell for going above and beyond the call of duty in his role as an editor for this monograph.

Library of Congress Cataloging in Publication Data

Goodman, John C.
    Social security in the United Kingdom.

    (AEI studies ; 335)
    1. Social Security—Great Britain. 2. Old age
pensions—Great Britain. I. Title. II. Series.
HD7165.G66   368.4′00941   81-10927
ISBN 0-8447-3460-8   AACR2

AEI Studies 335

Printed in the United States of America

Contents

FIGURES

Introduction

On April 6, 1978, citizens of the United Kingdom began participating in a new social security system. Workers fully participating in the system started to pay substantially higher payroll taxes—the total payroll tax jumped from 16.5 percent to 18.5 percent of covered wages. In return, these workers could expect larger pension benefits during their retirement.

Not all workers, however, are fully participating in the new system. The most interesting aspect of the British social security system is a provision that allows some workers to opt out—or, in British terminology, to *contract out*—of part of the program. Workers participating in an approved private pension plan are able to substitute their private pension for part of the social security pension. During their working years, those workers pay lower social security taxes than those paid by workers who fully participate in the system. In return, they will receive smaller social security benefits. The British system of contracting out is unique among the social security programs of Western industrialized countries.

Chapter 1 traces the historical development of welfare policy in Great Britain from the poor laws to the present system of retirement insurance. The new national pension system that began in 1978 is described in chapter 2. Chapter 3 explains the policy of contracting out and the advantages of doing so—higher rates of return are possible in private pensions than in social security. Chapter 5 summarizes the effects of the policy of contracting out.

1

From the Means Test to Retirement Insurance

Britain's current social security system is the result of gradual changes in its welfare policies over a very long period of time. The evolution has involved three principal stages. In stage 1, the approach taken was that of conventional welfare—need had to be established to obtain benefits. This stage lasted over several centuries under the British poor law. In stage 2, conventional welfare was replaced by social insurance in which benefits were given as a matter of right. Under the guidance of Lord Beveridge, this approach attempted to insure all citizens, including retirees, against the contingency of poverty and destitution. Stage 3 involved the explicit adoption of genuine retirement insurance. Under this approach, social security did more than simply insure the retiree against impoverishment. It also replaced a portion of past earnings and thereby took on more of the characteristics of a modern private pension plan.

The British Poor Law

Although the British welfare state is a relatively recent phenomenon, national concern with the problem of poverty dates back several centuries. The most important legislation came during the reign of Elizabeth I. The outcome was the infamous *Act for Reliefe of the Poore* of 1598. With a few modifications here and there, it remained the law of England until 1948.

The ostensible purpose of the law was precisely what its name implies: to provide for the relief of poverty-stricken individuals. Yet the method used to accomplish this objective implicitly recognized that the relief of poverty has important social dimensions.

For example, what if one family willingly chose to desert its dependent members, leaving them at the doorsteps of others? Or what if a whole community, through its refusal of relief, encouraged the "exportation" of its poor to neighboring communities? Alternatively, would not an especially generous family or community actually encourage the migration of beggars and alms-seekers from less generous surroundings? In each case, it is clear that the actions, or lack of them, by some people will have important effects on others.

Another problem concerns the effects of relief on the behavior of the recipients. Could not a continued source of support change the very character, and therefore the behavior, of an individual? Could it not encourage perpetual dependence at the expense of self-reliance and industry? If so, the relief of poverty could have damaging consequences both for the recipient of relief and for society as a whole.

The Elizabethan poor-law system was ideally designed to address these problems. It mitigated the first by spelling out precise liabilities for the care of the poor. The family of an applicant for relief, for example, was held to have a legal liability for the care and relief of that person if it possessed adequate financial means. In fact, the *means test* in England was originally a device to enforce family contributions for relief of the poor. Beyond the family, the liability fell to the local community in which the applicant had lived.

The law addressed the second problem through the principle of *less eligibility*. This principle stipulated that the conditions of public relief be such that the position of the relieved be kept below that of the poorest independent worker. It was enforced by insisting that most recipients of relief accept it by living in one of three houses, each reflecting the category into which the recipient fell. For the "impotent," there were "abiding places," or "poorhouses." For the "able-bodied" unemployed, there were "workhouses." For "unregenerate idlers," there were "houses of correction."[1] In addition to these forms of "indoor relief," there were provisions for "outdoor relief" for the working poor who were not living in workhouses.

The principle of less eligibility was not always adhered to. It appears that, physically, workhouses were often a better place to live than the alternative that many independent workers could afford. Nonetheless, anyone who came to the workhouse had to surrender to a number of rules and regulations that in retrospect seem quite harsh. In the workhouse, for example, workhouse clothes were required. There was no smoking or beer drinking. Silence was preserved at all meals. Families were separated (no sex). In general, no visitors were allowed. Residents were also disfranchised.

[1] See Maurice Bruce, *The Coming of the Welfare State* (London: B.T. Batsford, 1961), p. 41.

4

These restrictions satisfied an important intent behind the poor law: No one should be encouraged to seek relief if other options were available. Conditions for the acceptance of relief were such that they would ordinarily be refused by all but the most impoverished. In effect, acceptance of relief would prove the validity of the claim of destitution.

On the whole, the poor-law system was quite successful. It undoubtedly provided millions of poverty-stricken persons with adequate food and shelter. It was a truly comprehensive national system of welfare, and it accomplished its objectives in a way that minimized the social problems that threaten to attend any attempt at the relief of poverty.[2]

The poor-law system is not one of Britain's revered institutions, however. In part this is due to a bad press. The worst aspects of the system were publicized through the novels of Charles Dickens, Arnold Bennett, John Galsworthy, and others.[3] Typical of the spirit of the literary rebukes of the system is George Landsbury's grim account of a visit to the Poplar Workhouse in 1892:

> . . . going down the narrow land, ringing the bell, waiting while an official with a not too pleasant face looked through a grating to see who was there, and hearing his unpleasant voice . . . made it easy for me to understand why the poor dreaded and hated these places. . . . It was not necessary to write up the words "Abandon hope all ye who enter here" . . .; everything possible was done to inflict mental and moral degradation . . . of goodwill, kindliness, there was none.[4]

The literary accounts were not entirely exaggeration. The poor law may have been humanitarian in effect, but it was harsh in application.

Although the law distinguished three classes of poor, both in conditions for relief and in quarters, in practice they were often grouped under one heading and one roof. This meant that the truly impotent poor were often treated in the same way as the able-bodied poor. Moreover, the treatment generally amounted to contempt. A common attitude was that the able-bodied poor were deserving of

---

[2] The system discouraged dependence. From 1850 to the beginning of World War I, the percentage of the population on relief was nearly halved. See Ioan Gwilym Gibbon, "The Public Social Services," *Journal of the Royal Statistical Society*, part 4 (1937), p. 527.

[3] In *Our Mutual Friend*, Dickens went so far as to portray a character preferring to face starvation rather than seek relief.

[4] Quoted in Bruce, *The Coming of the Welfare State*, pp. 92–93.

moral reproach. John Locke, for example, in a report prepared for the Board of Trade in 1697 attributed the burden of pauperism to "the relaxation of discipline and corruption of manners" and proposed to discipline the poor by "the restraint of their debauchery . . . by suppressing the superfluous brandyshops and unnecessary ale houses."[5]

These views were echoed over a century later in the report of the 1832 commission that ascribed dependence on poor relief to "indolence, improvidence or vice" and advised that it "might have been averted by ordinary care and industry."[6] The same viewpoint was common among private charity organizations of the day. Charles S. Loch, secretary of the Charity Organization Society, one of the most important private charities at the turn of the century, wrote that "want of employment in nine cases out of ten in which the plea is used is not the cause of distress. It is, as often as not, drink."[7]

The acceptance of relief, therefore, tended to imply moral failing. Those who received aid were often assumed to be guilty of sin, laziness, and improvidence. Moreover, since this view was held not only by the well-to-do but by the working classes as well, it is no doubt true, as Bentley Gilbert has argued, that a great many workers lived in fear of the workhouse. That is, they lived with the fear that some misfortune might suddenly throw them onto poor-law relief.[8]

In fact, the term "poor law" and its attendant "means test" have become such phrases of abuse that all twentieth-century social welfare legislation has been affected by the legacy. Not only has it affected official policy, it also appears to weigh heavily upon the behavior of people who are poor today. A great many people are said to refuse to accept means-tested welfare benefits for which they qualify precisely because they are means-tested.[9]

Friendly Societies

So far, we have said nothing about the plight of the aged under the poor-law system. That is because prior to the turn of the century the

[5] Quoted in ibid., p. 33.

[6] Quoted in ibid., p. 80. An illustration of the official attitude toward the recipients of poor-law relief is the fact that of the 362 pages in the Poor Law Report of the Commission published in 1834, only 1 page was devoted to the "impotent" poor. The remainder was devoted to the "able-bodied."

[7] Quoted in Bentley B. Gilbert, *The Evolution of National Insurance in Great Britain: The Origins of the Welfare State* (London: Michael Joseph, 1966), pp. 51–52.

[8] Ibid., pp. 21–22.

[9] This is especially true of old people. See Anthony B. Atkinson, *Poverty in Britain and the Reform of Social Security* (Cambridge: Cambridge University Press, 1969), pp. 55–59.

normal assumption was that a man would work until he died. Aged workers, then, were just like other workers. They were expected to apply for relief only if they became sick and unable to work.[10]

During the nineteenth century, however, a great many workers were privately insured against loss of employment due to illness. Moreover, since loss of employment due to illness often correlated positively with age, the sick pay provided by private insurance often amounted to a retirement pension. In this way, many workers were able to provide for their own relief during their retirement years and avoid the dreaded poorhouse.

The main vehicle for the availability of such insurance was the *friendly society*. By the end of the nineteenth century, friendly societies had formed a vast network over Great Britain. In 1891, for example, it is believed that membership totaled from 4.25 to 4.5 million. That represents more than half of the adult males in the United Kingdom (England, Wales, and Scotland) for that year.[11]

Friendly societies often had many of the aspects of a fraternal lodge. Many of their charters emphasized the principles of Victorian morality and character development. Some were open only to members of a certain religious sect. Others were open only to teetotalers. Membership was generally confined to skilled workers and rarely included the very wealthy or the very poor.

The economic importance of the friendly societies derives from their role as private insurance companies. A typical worker, for example, would pay four to six pence per week in contributions. In return, he received medical care (usually under a contract), a death benefit, and sick pay amounting to ten shillings per week. The sum was adequate but hardly lavish.

Unfortunately, at the peak of their membership, a good many friendly societies were experiencing financial difficulties. The reason was that the contribution and benefit rates set for most of them were based on actuarial rates that had become outdated. Improvements in medical technology and more sanitary living conditions dramatically extended the life of the average British worker in the last quarter of the nineteenth century. As a consequence, the friendly societies found that their obligations exceeded their assets.

In addition, almost half of British workers did not have private insurance covering sick pay. The two factors combined provided an important impetus to the growing movement for a government pen-

---

[10] In the nineteenth century, very few workers reached today's pensionable age. In 1861, for example, less than 5 percent of the population was sixty-five years of age or older. By 1971, the share had climbed to about 13 percent.

[11] See Gilbert, *The Evolution of National Insurance*, p. 167.

sion policy in the first decade of the twentieth century. Whether for these reasons or the more cynical one—that government pensions were a method of buying votes—in 1908 the British government, for the first time, promised to pay an old age pension.[12]

The Old Age Pension Act of 1908

The act of 1908 promised a pension of five shillings per week to all men and women over the age of seventy. There was a means test, however. To qualify for a full pension, a recipient could not have income exceeding twenty-one pounds per year (about eight shillings per week). Above that amount, the recipient received a reduced pension, on a sliding scale. No pension was paid to anyone with an income equal to or greater than £31 10s.

Certain other conditions also had to be satisfied. The applicant had to prove that he had not been to prison within ten years (later changed to two years); that he was not a lunatic; that he was not receiving poor relief; and that he had been habitually employed in the trade of his choice. A large number of persons were eligible for the new old age pensions. In 1909, about 580,000 people began drawing such pensions, for a total of about £7.5 million.[13]

In retrospect, the act of 1908 does not as such represent a serious break with the British poor-law tradition. True, the pension was paid to the able-bodied as well as to the impotent and thus, as was claimed at the time, tended to discourage productive labor among those more than seventy years of age. At the same time, the means test ensured that the pension would only be paid to low-income individuals. Moreover, it was widely believed that these pensions would be largely a replacement for poor-law relief. Some evidence to support this belief is provided by the statistics on poor-law relief at the time. In 1906, there were 168,096 persons over the age of seventy not living in workhouses on outdoor relief. By 1913, this number had dropped to 8,563. Among those in workhouses on indoor relief, the effects were not as pronounced—61,378 in 1906 and 49,207 in 1913.[14] The pension of five shillings per week was the same as the estimated cost of maintaining a pauper in the workhouse.[15] The cost of outdoor relief was about one-half that amount.[16]

[12] Technically, an old age pension differs from a retirement pension in that the former establishes age alone as a condition for eligibility, whereas the latter establishes retirement in addition to age as the condition for eligibility.

[13] See Arthur Seldon, *The Great Pension "Swindle"* (London: Tom Stacey, 1970), p. 55.

[14] Gilbert, *The Evolution of National Insurance,* p. 229.

[15] Ibid., p. 216.

[16] Ibid., p. 228.

The Act of 1925

Although the act of 1908 did not make serious inroads on the British poor-law philosophy, two other programs developed several years later did. Compulsory health insurance was begun in 1912, and unemployment insurance was begun in a few industries in 1912 and expanded generally in 1920. In both of these areas, the principle of "social insurance" was applied. Taxes levied on employees and employers were said to "pay for" the benefits received. In effect, the state compelled a pooling of risks, and this practice was quite different from the traditional "dole."

The same principle was extended to old age pensions in the act of 1925. By that time, the old age pension was ten shillings per week for persons more than seventy who satisfied the means test.[17] Under the 1925 act, the same weekly pension would be paid to all men and women over the age of sixty-five, with no means test and no reduction in pension for existing income.

The pension was "paid for" by weekly contributions—9 pence for men and 4.5 pence for women—and was nominally shared equally by employer and employee. Covered benefits included widows' pensions and orphans' pensions in addition to the old age pension.

Since the state began paying such pensions only three years later (in 1928), it was somewhat ludicrous to maintain, as was done at the time, that retiring workers had "paid for" their own pensions. Nonetheless, had the backers of the act admitted that the earlier pensions paid under the plan were in fact a form of welfare financed by general taxation, it is possible that the act would not have passed. Such was the influence on British thinking of the poor-law system.

The Beveridge Plan

The National Assistance Act of 1948 opened dramatically with the statement that "the existing poor law shall cease to have effect." If there had been a truth-in-labeling law for acts of Parliament, the statement would certainly have called for some investigation. A great deal of what was previously done under the poor law simply continued under a different name—*national assistance*. For certain types of relief, the means test was still required.

Two important changes were made. First, administration of the relief for the poor was transferred from local authorities to the Na-

---

[17] The amount of the pension had been raised from five shillings per week to ten shillings per week in 1920.

tional Assistance Board. This meant that a uniform national scale for determining relief payments replaced the widely varying scales of local communities. Second, although persons accepting relief still had to satisfy a means test, the "household" means test was abolished. No longer were people legally liable for the financial support of members of their family.

A more important change, however, was reflected in the spirit of the times. The act of 1948 was the last of a series of measures passed by Parliament implementing the proposals of Sir William Beveridge. The Beveridge plan had been accepted in principle by the government in 1943. And if the objectives of the plan had been pursued over the following years, the poor law and the means test would indeed have ceased to exist.

Beveridge had two principal objectives: (1) to ensure for every citizen a minimum level of income and (2) to do so without the use of a means test. To accomplish these objectives, Beveridge sought a comprehensive and unified system of social insurance. Under the system, each citizen would make contributions in return for the guarantee at all times of a subsistence income for himself and his family as a matter of right.[18]

Under the Beveridge plan, any number of contingencies (unemployment, sickness, widowhood, industrial injuries, retirement, even the raising of children) would be covered by compulsory social insurance. Moreover, benefits would be received in the knowledge that, unlike the dole, they had been "paid for" through taxes on the worker's earnings.

The retirement pension scheme in existence at the time already satisifed Beveridge's notion of social insurance with two exceptions. First, Beveridge argued that a retirement pension, rather than an old age pension, should be paid at the age of sixty-five for men and sixty for women. Second, Beveridge argued that the existing pension was inadequate.

Accordingly, the National Insurance Act of 1946 succeeded in making the pension conditional on retirement. In addition the contribution and benefit rates were increased. The weekly pension benefit was raised from ten shillings to twenty-six shillings in 1946, and by 1948 the tax rate had reached four shillings, seven pence for men and three shillings, seven pence for women.

British pension policy under the Beveridge plan was not retirement insurance but rather an income maintenance system providing

[18] William Henry Beveridge, *Social Insurance and Allied Services* (New York: Macmillan, 1942), p. 7.

10

an income floor. Beveridge had hoped that the retirement pension would eventually rise to a level that was equal to, or greater than, the subsistence level of income to which he thought all British citizens were entitled. In that case, the pension would insure each worker against the possibility that he would be impoverished at retirement.

Because pension benefits were to provide a floor, they as well as other "social insurance" benefits were *flat-rate benefits*—the amount paid per week was a fixed sum, independent of the recipient's income or wealth. Since all citizens in equal circumstances were entitled to the same flat-rate benefits, all paid the same amount in contributions. Accordingly, "social insurance" contributions were also *flat-rate contributions*, independent of income or wealth.

Social security programs in most industrialized countries do not provide flat-rate benefits at retirement as in the Beveridge Plan. They are typically *earnings related*—the higher the preretirement earnings, the higher the amount of the pensions. Similarly, social security payroll taxes are also typically earnings related—the higher the worker's income, the higher the total tax.

It was probably inevitable that the British would eventually adopt an earnings-related pension program. Such a program was enacted in 1959 and went into effect in 1961. Earnings-related pensions in Britain, however, turned out to be quite unique.

The Act of 1959

In the act of 1959, earnings-related pensions were adopted as a "second tier," and earnings-related taxes were paid in addition to flat-rate taxes. The amount of the weekly flat-rate tax, the earnings-related tax rates, and the benefits per week in effect in September 1971 are shown in tables 1–3. Employees who were not contracted out and had earnings above £18 a week paid a lower tax rate than employees with lower earnings. Nonetheless, each £1 of taxes paid earned the same return at retirement: For every £7.5 of taxes, a worker could expect to receive an addition to his weekly pension of six pence (£.025).

A second feature of the 1959 legislation was even more novel. The government allowed workers to opt out of the earnings-related part of the system if they were participating in a private pension plan that promised benefits at least as good as those in the social security system.

The choice to opt out was actually not left to the individual worker. In order for one worker to opt out, all workers participating in the same private pension system had to opt out as well. None-

TABLE 1

WEEKLY FLAT-RATE TAX RATES PAID BY EMPLOYERS AND EMPLOYEES, 1971
(pounds)

	Amount of Tax	
Category	Employee not contracted out	Employee contracted out
Male		
Employee	0.88	1.00
Employer	2.15	2.27
Total	3.03	3.27
Female		
Employee	0.75	0.83
Employer	1.40	1.48
Total	2.15	2.31

SOURCE: Government Statistical Service, *Annual Abstract of Statistics*, 1976 (London: HMSO, 1976), pp. 62–64.

theless, the ability to contract out of part of the national insurance system amounted to a form of voluntary social security—a distinct departure from compulsory social insurance as envisioned by Beveridge.

Tables 1–3 show that contracted-out employees pay slightly higher flat-rate taxes. Nonetheless, they avoid paying earnings-related taxes, and they also give up the earnings-related benefits provided by the national insurance system.

Contracting out was not viewed in a favorable light by all sectors of British society. A number of critics, particularly those in the Labour party, viewed contracted-out workers as being in a privileged position. The point was not pushed to its ultimate conclusion, however. Few British politicians are willing to admit that the national insurance system offers a worse "deal" than that offered by private insurance. Nonetheless, the existence of private pensions, much like the existence of private education or private medical care, was at variance with the egalitarian aspirations of British socialists.

The upshot was a seesaw political battle over national pension policy that in many ways resembled the seesaw policy shifts over the nationalization of the steel industry.[19] Each party did its best to

[19] See Martin B. Tracy, "Social Security Revision in the United Kingdom," *Social Security Bulletin*, November 1975, pp. 32–49.

TABLE 2

EARNINGS-RELATED TAX RATES FOR EMPLOYEES
NOT CONTRACTED OUT, 1971
(percent)

| | Tax Rate | | |
Earnings Range	Employee	Employer	Total
£ 9–£18	4.75	4.75	9.50
£18–£42	4.35	4.35	8.70

SOURCE: Government Statistical Service, *Annual Abstract of Statistics*, 1976, pp. 62, 64.

TABLE 3

WEEKLY BENEFITS, 1971
(pounds)

Category	Amount
Flat rate	
Single person	6.00
Married couple	9.70
Earnings related (for employees not contracted out)	.025 for each 7.5 contribution

SOURCE: Government Statistical Service, *Annual Abstract of Statistics*, 1976, pp. 62, 64.

undo the program of the previous party in power. The objective of the Labour party was to reduce, or perhaps eliminate altogether, the role of private pensions in Britain. The Conservative party's objective was the opposite—to increase the role of private pensions, perhaps to the point of eliminating the national insurance system. The Labour party's pension policy during the three years preceding 1978 contrasted sharply with the new pension program—contracting out was abolished, flat-rate contributions were abolished, and earnings-related benefits were abolished. What was left was a system with earnings-related contributions and flat-rate benefits, in which a worker had to earn a minimum income level before he was liable for any taxes and in which there was a maximum amount of income taxed.

The new pension system was finally agreed to by leaders of both

13

parties in 1975. It became effective on April 6, 1978. Like the system that lasted from 1961 to 1975, the new national pension program has two tiers, and workers are allowed to contract out of the second tier.

2

The New National Pension System, 1978

When the white paper outlining the government's proposal for a new national pension system was published in 1974, payroll tax rates in Britain were lower than those in many industrialized European countries.[1] Also, retirement pensions were failing to meet the Beveridge objective of providing a minimum income to all retirees without means-tested benefits. A major change in the new program was the enactment of higher payroll taxes and higher retirement benefits.

Payroll Taxes

The social security tax in Britain, as in many countries, is nominally divided between the employer and the employee. The bulk of the recent increase in payroll tax rates consisted of the employer's "share" of the tax. From 1975 to 1978, the employee's tax rate increased from 5.5 percent to 6.5 percent of salary; the employer's tax rate jumped from 8.5 percent to 12 percent of salary. The combined tax rate was thus increased from 14 percent to 18.5 percent.

Most economists attach little significance to the division of the total payroll tax into employee and employer shares. In the United States, the employee pays income taxes on his share of the payroll tax, whereas he does not pay income taxes on the employer's share. Beyond that, the nominal division of the tax between employer and employee tells us nothing about who bears the ultimate burden.

Although there may be industry variations, the evidence suggests that on the average the burden of the U.S. payroll tax falls on employees.[2] This means that if the total combined payroll tax were 12 percent of salary, the average worker's income would have been

---

[1] Martin B. Tracy, "Payroll Taxes under Social Security Programs: Cross-National Survey," *Social Security Bulletin*, December 1975, pp. 3–15.

[2] See John A. Brittain, *The Payroll Tax for Social Security* (Washington, D.C.: The Brookings Institution, 1972).

about 12 percent higher in the absence of the tax. The entire increase in social security taxes in Britain from 1975 to 1978 probably came at the expense of the workers themselves.

Maximum and Minimum Earnings Limits. The British payroll tax applies only to income up to a maximum earnings limit (stated in terms of weekly salary). The maximum earnings limit is equal to about one and one-half times the average salary of a male blue-collar worker and is revised periodically as average wages increase. In 1978, the maximum earnings limit was £120.00 per week.

The British payroll tax also has a *minimum earnings limit.* Persons with incomes below this limit are not liable for payroll taxes. The minimum earnings limit is equal to approximately one-seventh of the maximum earnings limit and, like the maximum earnings limit, is revised periodically to reflect the increase in average wages. In 1978, the minimum earnings limit was £17.50 per week.

The minimum earnings limit provides tax relief for low-income workers. Because workers who make less than the minimum earnings limit usually qualify for supplementary welfare benefits, it is argued that taxes on workers with very low incomes would, in any event, probably be returned through supplementary benefits.

Incentive Effects of the Tax. A disadvantage of the minimum earnings limit is its effect on work incentives. Consider a worker earning £16.50 per week. Because his income is below the minimum earnings limit, he would pay no social security tax. If he earns £1 more per week, his weekly income reaches the minimum earnings limit, and his *entire* weekly earnings are now subject to the social security payroll tax. At a total tax rate of 18.5 percent, this means that in return for earning £1 more per week, the worker pays taxes equal to £3.24 per week—a tax rate of 324 percent! In order to be just as well off as he was when he earned only £16.50 per week, he would have to earn £20.25. His gross salary must increase about 23 percent in order to avoid a loss of real income.

It is surprising that the incentive effects of the minimum earnings limit have received so little attention in Britain, in view of the considerable attention given to the incentive effects of supplementary benefits.[3] The disincentives to work because of supplementary ben-

---

[3] See Hugh Herbert, "Supplementary Benefits 'Cannot Rise Ahead of Basic Incomes,' " (Manchester) *Guardian,* September 15, 1977; and *Report of the Supplementary Benefits Commission for 1976* (London: HMSO, 1977).

efits are probably much less than those resulting from the effect of the minimum earnings limit on marginal social security tax rates.

In the future, the incentive effects of the minimum earnings limit will probably be greater than in the past because of the rise in payroll tax rates. Also, wives may now find part-time employment in low-paying jobs less attractive than formerly because they can no longer opt for voluntary participation in social security.

Regressivity of the Tax. For fully participating workers earning above the minimum earnings limit, taxes are a constant proportion of income up to the maximum earnings limit. Above the maximum earnings limit, taxes are a declining proportion of income. For example, a fully participating worker earning £100 per week pays social security taxes equal to 18.5 percent of income, whereas a similar worker earning £200 per week pays taxes equal to 11 percent of income, and at £300 per week, payroll taxes are only 7 percent of income. As is the case with the U.S. payroll tax, for persons with incomes above the maximum earnings limit, British social security taxes are regressive with respect to income.

Tax Rates for Wage Earners, the Self-Employed, and Voluntary Contributors. Table 4 shows the tax rates and flat-rate taxes applicable to different classes of persons in 1977 and 1978. Wage and salary earners are included in Class 1 contributors, and the great bulk of social security taxes are paid by them.

Class 2 and Class 4 contributions are those paid by the self-employed. Class 2 covers their flat-rate contributions, and their Class 4 contributions are roughly based on the amount of their income between the lower and upper earnings limit. The self-employed fare even better in Britain than in the United States. As shown in table 4, in 1977, British self-employed workers paid about 8 percent of income up to the maximum—a little less than one-half of the total combined payroll tax imposed on Class 1 employees and their employers.[4] Self-employed workers in the United States pay taxes that have usually been three-fourths the combined tax rate paid by other workers and their employers. The British treatment of self-employed persons became even more favorable in 1978. A self-employed

[4] A British self-employed worker earning the maximum earnings limit in 1977 would pay about 2.6 percent of income as a Class 2 contributor and about 5.4 percent of income as a Class 4 contributor. A self-employed worker earning the minimum earnings limit in 1977 would pay about 8 percent of income as a Class 2 contributor and no taxes as a Class 4 contributor.

TABLE 4

PAYROLL TAX RATES BEFORE AND AFTER THE INTRODUCTION OF THE NEW NATIONAL PENSION SYSTEM

Class	April 1977	April 1978
Class 1: employees (percent)		
Employee's tax rate[a]	5.75	6.50
Employer's tax rate[b]	10.75	12.00
Total tax rate	16.50	18.50
Class 2: self-employed (pounds)		
Flat-rate tax per week for		
Males	2.66	1.90
Females	2.55	1.90
Class 3: voluntary contribution (pounds)		
Flat-rate tax per week	2.45	1.80
Class 4: self-employed		
Tax rate	8% of income for £1,750–£5,500 per year	5% of income for £2,000–£6,250 per year

[a] Rate is applicable to employees whose weekly earnings are at least equal to £15 in 1977 and £17.50 in 1978.
[b] Includes 2 percent surcharge paid to the treasury.
SOURCE: Government Statistical Service, *Annual Abstract of Statistics*, 1979, pp. 65, 67.

worker earning the maximum earnings limit in 1978 paid about 5 percent of his income in social security taxes—less than one-third the combined taxes paid on the salary of an employee.[5]

Benefits are also lower for self-employed workers, however. Under the new pension system, self-employed workers are entitled to a basic flat-rate pension at retirement but are not entitled to an earnings-related pension. On the other hand, British tax law includes a provision similar to the U.S. Keogh plan. Self-employed persons can set aside 15 percent of gross income, up to a maximum amount, in a private retirement fund and claim an income tax deduction. As shown in table 4, prior to 1978, Class 2 contribution rates on the self-employed differed for men and women. Under the new state pension scheme, this differential is eliminated.

[5] As a Class 2 contributor, he would pay about 1.6 percent of his income; and as a Class 4 contributor, he would pay about 3.4 percent of his income.

British workers who fail to earn the minimum earnings limit or who are unemployed for a substantial period of time can make voluntary contributions to safeguard certain benefit rights (mainly retirement pensions). These contributions are called Class 3 contributions and are a flat-rate tax. The new system preserves this feature of British social security, although the weekly contribution is set at about 70 percent of its previous level. The social security system in the United States does not have provisions of this type.

Benefits

The new social security system has two tiers of pension benefits. The first tier is a flat-rate pension called the *basic component pension*. The second tier is an earnings-related pension called the *additional component pension*.

The Basic Flat-Rate Pension. All single workers whose average preretirement income is equal to or more than the minimum earnings limit receive a weekly flat-rate pension. In April 1978 this pension was equal to the minimum earnings limit (£17.50 per week). The pension will be raised periodically to reflect the increase in prices and will be paid to all workers who satisfy the retirement test when they reach the eligibility age (sixty-five for men and sixty for women).

For retired male workers with a dependent spouse, the basic component pension is increased roughly 60 percent. If the wife is entitled to a pension in her own right, as in the United States, she cannot collect both her own pension as a retired worker and a dependent's pension based on her husband's earnings.

For most workers, the calculation of the flat-rate pension is the same as it was under the interim pension system from April 1975 to April 1978. For those workers whose preretirement income averages less than the minimum earnings limit, however, there is an important change. Under the old system, a worker had to qualify for the flat-rate pension in order to receive any pension. Under the new system, low-income workers will be entitled to a pension equal to one pound for each pound of earnings up to the minimum earnings limit (100 percent of their preretirement earnings).

The Additional Component Pension. The additional component pension is based on earnings between the two earnings limits: For each year of employment under the new program, a worker is entitled to a weekly earnings-related pension of 1.25 percent (one-eightieth) of earnings above the lower earnings limit up to the upper earnings limit. A worker who earns an income less than or equal to the minimum earnings limit in any given year receives no additional component pension for that year. On the other hand, a worker who earns an income equal to or greater than the maximum earnings limit in any given year receives an additional component pension equal to 1.25 percent of the entire difference between the upper and lower earnings limits.

The new pension system is scheduled to grow to maturity over a period of twenty years—the maximum number of years on which the earnings-related pension can be calculated. A worker who retires on the day the system reaches maturity (April 6, 1998) will receive an earnings-related pension equal to 25 percent (20 × 1.25) of average preretirement earnings between the two earnings limits.[6]

For those who work more than twenty years under the new system, the additional component pension is limited to 25 percent of average earnings between the two earnings limits. Such workers will usually benefit, however, because their pensions will be calculated on the basis of the twenty years in which earnings were highest.

Both the flat-rate pension and the earnings-related pension are indexed to provide protection against inflation. The earnings history of each worker on which the earnings-related pension is calculated is also indexed.

Amounts Paid to a Retiree. For an example of how a worker's total pension is calculated, consider the case of a married male worker who retires one year after the system began. If his average weekly salary in his last year before retirement is £60, his pension (based on April 1978 values) would amount to £28.53, according to this calculation:

Basic components	£17.50
Additional component	
[1.25 percent of (£60 − £17.50)]	0.53
Wife's pension	
(on husband's contribution alone)	10.50
Total	£28.53

[6] The 25 percent rule applies only to workers whose income never exceeds the maximum earnings limit. If a worker earns more than the maximum earnings limit in one or two years, he is not allowed to carry over surplus income from those years and apply it to years when income was lower. Similarly, a worker who earns more than the maximum earnings limit in every year would receive an additional component pension equal to only 25 percent of the difference between the two earnings limits— an amount equal to about 21 percent of the maximum earnings limit.

TABLE 5

Replacement Rate of Retirement Pensions under New and Interim Pension Systems after Ten Years of Operation

| | Interim System[a] | | New System | |
Weekly Earnings (£)	Amount of flat-rate pension (£)	Percentage of earnings	Amount of flat-rate and earnings-related pension (£)	Percentage of earnings
Single person				
20	17.50	88	17.81	89
40	17.50	44	20.30	51
60	17.50	29	22.80	38
80	17.50	22	25.30	32
100	17.50	18	27.81	28
120	17.50	15	30.31	25
Married couple[b]				
20	28.00	140	28.31	142
40	28.00	70	30.80	77
60	28.00	47	33.30	56
80	28.00	35	35.80	45
100	28.00	28	38.31	38
120	28.00	23	40.81	34

NOTE: These figures are based on earnings levels in April 1978. In April 1978, the lower earnings limit was £17.50; the upper earnings limit was £120.00; the basic component pension was £17.50 for a single person and £28.00 for a couple. The average wage paid to a male blue-collar worker was approximately £80.00.
[a] The Interim Pension System was in effect from April 1975 to April 1978.
[b] Based on husband's record alone.
SOURCE: Author.

Table 5 (for ten years of employment) and table 6 (for twenty years of employment) show examples of worker's pensions under the flat-rate pension in the interim system from 1975 to 1978 and under the new system with flat-rate and earnings-related pensions.[7] The values in these tables are expressed in constant 1978 values, and no allowance is made for inflation.

Consider the case of a married male blue-collar worker earning the average wage in 1978—about £80.00 per week. Tables 5 and 6

[7] Tables 5 and 6 ignore the indexing problem.

TABLE 6

REPLACEMENT RATE OF RETIREMENT PENSIONS UNDER NEW AND
INTERIM PENSION SYSTEMS AFTER TWENTY YEARS OF OPERATION

| | Interim System[a] | | New System | |
Weekly Earnings (£)	Amount of flat-rate pension (£)	Percent of earnings	Amount of flat-rate and earnings-related pension (£)	Percent of earnings
Single person				
20	17.50	88	18.13	91
40	17.50	44	23.13	58
60	17.50	29	28.13	47
80	17.50	22	33.13	41
100	17.50	18	38.13	38
120	17.50	15	43.13	36
Married couple[b]				
20	28.00	140	28.63	143
40	28.00	70	33.63	84
60	28.00	47	38.63	64
80	28.00	35	43.63	55
100	28.00	28	48.63	49
120	28.00	23	53.63	45

NOTE: These figures are based on earnings levels in April 1978. In April 1978, the lower earnings limit was £17.50; the upper earnings limit was £120.00; the basic component pension was £17.50 for a single person and £28.00 for a couple. The average wage paid to a male blue-collar worker was approximately £80.00.
[a] The Interim Pension System was in effect from April 1975 to April 1978.
[b] Based on husband's record alone.
SOURCE: Author.

show that he would have retired on a pension equal to about 35 percent of preretirement earnings had the interim flat-rate pension system been continued. Under the new system with both flat-rate and earnings-related pensions, he will receive 45 percent of earnings after ten years of employment; and after twenty years of employment, the pension received by him and his wife will be 55 percent of earnings.

Distributional Effects of the New Pension System. Instead of increasing benefits as shown in tables 5 and 6, the government could have increased benefits by raising the flat-rate pension that existed under the interim pension plan. If the flat-rate pension payable to a couple had been increased from £28.00 to £43.63, for example, the average worker earning £80 a week would have been just as well off. Under either system, he would have retired with a pension equal to 55 percent of earnings.

Extending the flat-rate pension would have made an enormous difference to workers at other income levels, however. If the couple's flat-rate pension had been increased over a twenty-year period to £43.63, then all couples would have received £15.63 more per week as a result of the extension. In contrast, under the new system, a £20-per-week worker, after twenty years, receives a pension increase of only £0.63. On the other hand, the £120-per-week worker receives an additional component pension equal to £25.63. *The new state pension system substantially alters the distribution of social security benefits.* High-income workers will receive large increases in their weekly pensions, whereas low-income workers will receive very small increases.

To see the distributional effects of the new system more clearly, let us contrast the position of a worker who always earns the maximum earnings limit with a worker who always earns the minimum earnings limit. Since 1975, both workers have faced tax hikes equal to 4.5 percent of income. Yet the minimum-income earner receives no increase in pension benefits at retirement! In contrast, the maximum-income earner (with a dependent wife) receives a pension almost twice as large as the pension he otherwise would have received. The pension payable to a single maximum-income earner is *more* than twice as large as the pension he would otherwise have received.

Under the new system, however, pension benefits expressed as a percentage of previous earnings are still inversely related to income. At maturity, the system pays the £20 worker a pension equal to 143 percent of income. It pays the £120 worker a pension equal to 45 percent of income.

Treatment of Women

Under the new pension system, men and women pay identical tax rates and at retirement receive identical pensions if they have had similar earnings. Moreover, private pension plans (called "occupational" schemes) are now required to be open to men and women on the same terms. Conditions such as age of entry, length of service before becoming a member, and optional entry must apply equally to men and women employees.[8]

Although it was officially announced that one of the most significant features of the new system was "the right it gives to women to enjoy full equality with men," full equality has not been achieved.[9] The pensionable age is still sixty for women but sixty-five for men, and a woman still enjoys privileged treatment as a surviving spouse. It is not entirely clear that the new rules bring about greater equality of treatment for men and women than existed before.

Basic Conflict. As in the social security programs of other industrialized countries, there is in Britain a basic conflict over the treatment of women.[10] This conflict stems from the ambiguous role of social security itself: *Is social security primarily a welfare program, or is it primarily a retirement insurance program?*

Viewed as an insurance program, social security has as its primary function to insure the worker against the contingency that he will live beyond the retirement age. Social security meets this contingency by replacing a portion of earnings forgone when the worker retires. Moreover, the insurance principle requires that benefit payments be based on the taxes paid by the worker and his employer as well as on the mortality rates for various classes of workers.

Viewed as a welfare program, social security should primarily guarantee that the minimum financial needs of the elderly do not go unmet. Social security, according to this view, is an income transfer plan. The crucial determinant of benefit payments is need, not past contributions or actuarial probabilities of life expectancy. Moreover, the crucial determinant of taxes, according to this view, is ability to pay.

British social security, like its American counterpart, has never served either of these two functions exclusively. Instead, it has forged a middle position—it has been in part a welfare program and in part an insurance program. The two different concepts of social security have very different implications for the treatment of women.

Consider the problem of the dependent's pension for a married

[8] Some of these provisions were passed as early as 1975 in anticipation of the new system.

[9] "Government Launches New Pension Scheme," press release (London: Department of Health and Social Security, February 27, 1975), p. 1.

[10] For a survey of the treatment of women in the social security programs of other countries, see Robert W. Weise, "Housewives and Pensions: Foreign Experience," *Social Security Bulletin*, September 1976, pp. 27–45. For the role of women under the U.S. social security system, see Marilyn Flowers, *Women and Social Security: An Institutional Dilemma* (Washington, D.C.: American Enterprise Institute, 1977).

couple. Under the insurance concept, a worker would not receive a dependent's pension unless he had contributed an additional amount during his working years to pay for the extra pension. Moreover, if a wife qualifies for benefits in her own right, the couple would receive both the dependent's pension, if it has been paid for, and the pension she earned herself.

Under the welfare concept, if both spouses have adequate pensions in their own right, the needs of the family are presumedly being met. There would be no reason to pay a dependent's pension, since the need for the additional pension does not exist. If the wife does not qualify for benefits on her own, however, an unmet need exists, and this additional need would require a larger pension. Moreover, since taxes should be levied on the ability-to-pay principle, there is no reason, in setting payroll tax rates, to ask whether a worker is married, ever expects to be married or, if he is married, whether his wife is contributing to her own pension.

The Policy before 1975. Prior to 1975, women were entitled to a dependent's pension only if they had no pension in their own right, but married women workers were given a choice about whether to participate in social security. It seemed unfair to require women to pay social security taxes while their husbands were also paying taxes (thus ensuring their right to a dependent's pension). If they chose to participate, they paid the full payroll tax rate paid by male workers and became entitled to a pension in their own right. If they chose not to participate, they paid no social security taxes. Under the latter option, married women workers were still entitled to maternity, retirement, and survivors' benefits on the basis of their husband's contributions. Still, these benefits were smaller than those payable under full coverage. In addition, such women had to forgo the right to sickness, unemployment, and invalidism benefits.

In 1975, fewer than 1.2 million out of approximately 5 million married women workers chose to maintain independent coverage. This is hardly surprising. For the married woman worker, the gains from participation were not the full range of benefits ordinarily available to a male worker but the difference between the full range of benefits and the benefits that were available as a dependent. In addition, in order to qualify for a full retirement pension in their own right, married women had to satisfy the *half-test*—they had to pay social security taxes for at least one-half of the years between the date of their marriage and age sixty.[11]

[11] Under certain circumstances, married women are required to have more qualifying years than single women. See Weise, "Housewives and Pensions," p. 40.

The Policy after 1975. Because so few women volunteered to maintain independent insurance coverage, legislation was enacted in 1975, in line with the welfare concept, that eliminated the choice between independent and dependent coverage. Nonetheless, married women workers were still allowed to pay lower taxes—2 percent as compared with the usual 5.5 percent—in return for a smaller range of benefits. The full range of benefits included old age, invalidism, survivors', medical, sickness, maternity, work injury, and unemployment benefits. The reduced range of benefits provided only limited old age, maternity, medical, and survivors' benefits.

In accordance with the insurance concept, the 1975 law allowed a married woman who dropped out of the labor market and who had been paying the full 5.5 percent contribution rate to make a voluntary contribution and thereby keep her insurance record intact. Relatively few women chose this option. In 1975, only 200,000 married women made voluntary contributions.[12]

Prior to 1975, there were differences in the payroll tax rates paid by men and women. In January 1974, the total weekly flat-rate tax was £2.12 for male employees and £1.79 for female employees. The rationale given for this distinction was that the flat-rate benefit paid to women at retirement did not normally include a dependent's supplement, whereas the flat-rate benefit paid to men often did.[13] The differential payroll tax rates were consistent with the insurance concept.

On the other hand, women paid slightly higher *earnings-related* payroll taxes and received slightly lower earnings-related benefits. This was also defended on the insurance concept—women were allowed to retire earlier and on actuarial grounds were expected to live longer than men. Despite the provision for such benefits, less than one-fourth of women pensioners received an earnings-related benefit.[14]

Legislation enacted in 1975 eliminated these tax and benefit differentials and substituted a uniform payroll tax rate and a flat-rate benefit equally applicable to male and female employees. This legislation was in accordance with the welfare concept. In addition, the new pension system abolished the half-test for married women and

---

[12] Ibid.

[13] For a discussion of the motives behind the differential tax rates, see Dalmer Hoskins and Lenore Bixby, *Women and Social Security: Law and Policy in Five Countries,* Research Report 42, Office of Research and Statistics, Social Security Administration, 1973.

[14] See Weise, "Housewives and Pensions."

the right of married women to pay a lower, 2 percent tax rate in return for reduced benefits.[15]

Credits for Domestic Care. Under the new program both women and men may receive "credits" for years they spent raising children or caring for sick or elderly persons. These credits affect social security benefits in the following way: In order to be entitled to a full retirement pension, a worker must have a minimum number of qualifying years—thirty-nine years for women and forty-four years for men. A qualifying year is a year in which the worker's annual wage is at least equal to the annual minimum earnings limit.

As of April 1978, workers are able to substitute a certain number of years of domestic care for qualifying years and still preserve their pension rights. These are years during which the individual is raising a child under the age of sixteen or is spending a certain number of hours per week attending a sick or elderly person. In order to qualify for a full retirement pension, these workers must have at least twenty qualifying years during which social security taxes are paid.

The ability to receive credits for years of domestic care will be especially important to women. It is not certain, however, that most of them will find this provision to be more beneficial than the half-test, which the new provision replaces. Credits for child or sick care, moreover, are consistent with the welfare concept of social security.

Survivors. The new pension system enhances the ability of widows to inherit their husband's pensions. Prior to 1978, although a widow *under* the age of sixty received a flat-rate pension based on her husband's participation, she did not receive an additional pension based on her husband's earnings-related taxes. After reaching the age of sixty, she was entitled to one-half of her husband's earnings-related pension. These restrictions were consistent with the welfare concept.

A widow is now entitled to a portion of her husband's earnings-related pension *before* she reaches the age of sixty and, after that, 100 percent of her husband's pension. Moreover, if she is entitled to a pension in her own right, she will be able to combine her husband's pension with her own, subject to two qualifications: (1) The total flat-rate pension must not exceed the maximum flat-rate pension payable to a single person, and (2) the total earnings-related

[15] The right is retained for married women workers (and widows) who chose the 2 percent option prior to April 6, 1978. The right to pay the lower tax rate ends if there is a break in employment lasting for two consecutive income tax years.

pension must not exceed the maximum earnings-related pension payable to a single person. The liberalization under the new law is consistent with the insurance concept. The restrictions on the amount of pension that can be inherited are consistent with the welfare concept.

Unsolved Problems. In principle, social security can treat all workers equally under either the welfare concept or the insurance concept. Often, however, equality of treatment under one concept implies inequality of treatment under the other.

The social security system could deny all workers the right to draw both the pension one has paid for and a dependent's pension. This would be consistent with equality of treatment under the welfare concept. Yet such a rule would be inconsistent with the insurance concept. Given the present composition of the labor market, the primary victims of such a rule would be married women workers. Similarly, equality under the welfare concept implies that equal earnings should be equally taxed. Yet since expected benefits may be quite different for different people—on actuarial grounds—the equal-tax-for-equal-pay rule results in inequality of treatment under the insurance concept.

For this reason, many of the rules in force prior to 1975 may not have reflected discrimination based on sex as much as adherence to the insurance concept of social security. Even so, the older rules were not evenhanded. Options reserved for married women workers were not granted to male workers in similar circumstances. Moreover, actuarial distinctions only differentiated between men and women. They did not apply to different groups of male workers, as they would under private retirement insurance.[16] Nonetheless, older pension policy, on balance, adhered to the insurance point of view.

Similarly, most of the policy changes reflect a switch to the welfare concept of social security rather than any broad-based movement toward equal treatment of men and women. Indeed, for someone committed to the insurance concept of social security, most of the policy changes during the last three years do not create more equality.

Whether one views these changes as creating more or less equality between men and women, there is a more basic question to be asked: Do the changes in pension policy regarding women leave the average woman better off or worse off?

---

[16] Private pension funds make distinctions based on occupation, income, and perhaps other characteristics as well, insofar as these characteristics are predictors of mortality rates.

TABLE 7

TAXES AND PENSIONS FOR SINGLE AND MARRIED WOMEN WORKERS UNDER THE NEW PENSION SYSTEM AT MATURITY

Weekly Earnings (£)	Weekly Tax (£)	Net Weekly Pension (£)[a]	Ratio of Net Pension to Tax
Single women			
25	4.63	19.38	4.18
50	9.25	25.63	2.77
120	22.20	43.13	1.94
Married women			
25	4.63	8.88	1.92
50	9.25	15.13	1.64
120	22.20	32.63	1.47

[a] The net weekly pension for married women is equal to the pension received by a single woman on the basis of her own earnings less the dependent's pension received by wives.
SOURCE: Author.

In the early days of the national insurance system, there were few married working women in the labor market. Beveridge regarded the problem of what to do about married working women as minor,[17] and he advocated that they be permitted to remain outside the system. At that time, the most important policies affecting women were considered to be the provisions pertaining to survivorship rights.

In Britain half of all married couples under the retirement age currently have two wage earners, and it has been estimated that, on the average, the earnings of wives amount to about 25 percent of the total income of families.[18] Today, the most important features of pension policy affecting women are those that pertain to working wives.

How, then, does the working wife fare under the new pension system? Some clue to the plight of working wives is provided in table 7, which shows the weekly tax rates and pensions for single and married women workers at different income levels. A worker earning £20 per week earns just above the minimum earnings limit,

[17] Beveridge wrote: "The small minority of women who undertake paid employment or other gainful occupation after marriage . . . require special treatment differing from that of a single woman." See William Henry Beveridge, Social Insurance and Allied Services (New York: Macmillan, 1942), p. 50.
[18] Hilary Land, "Who Cares for the Family?" Journal of Social Policy, vol. 7, part 3 (July 1978), p. 261.

and a worker earning £120 per week earns the maximum earnings limit. The average wage received by women working full time in 1978 was about £50.

For a single woman worker, the entries are identical to those for a single man. For a married woman worker, there is an important difference. The calculations of the weekly pension for married women workers assume that the husband is the primary wage earner and that the wife would have been entitled to a dependent's pension.[19] This is true for 90 percent of all couples. The net weekly pension of a married woman worker is the single person's pension minus the dependent's pension that must be sacrificed if the wife draws a pension in her own right.

In table 7 the ratios of pension to tax provide an insight into the "return" that workers get on their "investment" in social security. For single women workers, the ratio of pension to tax is the same as it is for single male workers.[20] Moreover, the low-income (£25) single woman worker's ratio of pension to tax is about twice as large as that received by the high-income worker (£120).

Table 7 shows that the high-income single worker receives a better deal from social security than the married woman worker at almost every income level. *Also, a single woman worker with the highest earnings has approximately the same rate of pension to tax as married women earning very low incomes.* In addition, the "penalty" for being married is highest for women whose income is the lowest. Most women workers do not work full time. Of the 4.25 million part-time employees in 1975, 84 percent were women, and most of them were married.[21] Among married working women as a group, average income is probably between twenty and thirty pounds a week, although the average income of full-time women workers in 1978 was about fifty pounds.

It is ironic that so much acclaim has been given to the equality-of-treatment provisions of the new pension system. By abolishing the right of voluntary participation in the future and by further removing the 2 percent tax rate option for women, the government has almost certainly made a majority of working women worse off.[22]

There are also provisions of the new system that result in un-

[19] See Wise Nandy, "Double Bind for Women," *New Society*, September 28, 1978.

[20] The rate of return paid to male workers, however, is lower than that paid to women workers because women may retire five years earlier, and on the average they live five years longer than men.

[21] Land, "Who Cares for the Family?" p. 280.

[22] For some working women, provisions that benefit working women with children may offset these disadvantages.

equal treatment of men and women, regardless of which concept of social security is employed. For example, widows over age fifty (or any age, if they have dependent children) inherit the whole of their husband's pension. Widowers, by contrast, can inherit their spouse's pension only if they are retired, sick, or disabled. In addition, a retired widow is able to combine any pension based on her own earnings with one based on her husband's earnings as long as the combined pension does not exceed the maximum pension payable to a single person. A retired widower, however, can use his wife's earnings only in calculating his flat-rate pension unless his wife dies when both are over the pensionable age. A widow whose husband was contracted out of the pension system, however, receives a pension equal to at least one-half the guaranteed minimum pension, with the balance provided by the government. No similar provision exists for widowers.

Perhaps the most glaring form of inequality that exists under British social security is that of persons at the retirement age. Women are able to draw a retirement pension at age sixty, whereas men are not allowed to draw a pension until age sixty-five. This distinction is consistent with neither the welfare concept nor the insurance concept of social security. If men and women pay identical payroll taxes or identical income, the insurance concept would dictate a later retirement age for women than for men or a smaller benefit because of the longer life expectancy of women.

An important inquiry into the question of the proper eligibility age was made by the Occupational Pensions Board (OPB) under Lord Allen.[23] The Allen Report considered the insurance concept only briefly and then came down firmly on the side of welfare—there should be no difference in the eligibility ages of men and women. The report was concerned primarily with the law governing private pension plans and concluded that it would be ludicrous to require private pensions to treat men and women in the same way unless a similar provision were included in the national insurance system. The British government's policy of retaining different eligibility ages for men and women was presented to the Equal Opportunities Commission by David Ennals, secretary of state for social services.[24] The reason given was primarily political, but behind the politics of pensions lay some hard economic facts.

The pensionable age for women could be raised to sixty-five or

[23] See *Equal Status for Men and Women in Occupational Pension Schemes* (Allen Report)(London: HMSO, 1976).

[24] "Pension Ages for Men and Women," press release (London: Department of Health and Social Security, September 23, 1976).

the pensionable age for men could be lowered to sixty. The first option could have been disastrous politically. There was no pressure, even from women's rights organizations, to adopt it. The second option would probably have been politically popular, but it would have been very costly, and the higher taxes needed to meet these costs might have been politically impossible to impose.

Lowering the male retirement age to sixty would not only reduce payroll tax collections, but it would also boost the outflow of retirement pensions. The burden of paying the additional pensions would also fall on a smaller number of workers. Currently, the ratio of the population of working age to the population of pensionable age is about 3.5 to 1. It is estimated that lowering the retirement age for men to sixty would lower this ratio to 3 to 1.

It was estimated that the change would cost about £2 billion a year in 1976. This would represent about two pounds per week, on the average, per worker. The additional payroll tax needed was calculated to be about 4 percent of the average worker's wage.

Ennals also argued that lowering the male retirement age would have important effects on Britain's annual output of goods and services. The country's gross national product, he estimated, would decline by 3 to 4 percent.

Inflation-Proofing

As in most other industrialized countries, over the past several decades British pensions have been increased so as to maintain their real value.[25] The method of adjustment to inflation was originally largely ad hoc. Between 1950 and 1970, the government increased the flat-rate pension on the average every two and one-half years. The timing of the increase was usually political.[26] In six of the seven general elections between 1950 and 1970, there was a pension increase during the election year or the year immediately preceding it.

Figure 1 contrasts the rise in the flat-rate pension of a married couple with the rise in average wages and retail prices from 1961 to 1973. Despite the erratic rise in pension benefits, increases roughly kept pace with the increase in the average gross earning of a male

[25] See *Pensions and Inflation* (Geneva: International Labor Office, 1977), p. 2; and Martin B. Tracy, "Maintaining Value of Social Security Benefits during Inflation: Foreign Experience," *Social Security Bulletin*, November 1976, pp. 33–42.

[26] Laurence Lustgarten, "The Uprating Scandal," *New Society*, November 4, 1976, pp. 251–52.

FIGURE 1
RETIREMENT PENSIONS, EARNINGS,
AND RETAIL PRICES, 1961–1973

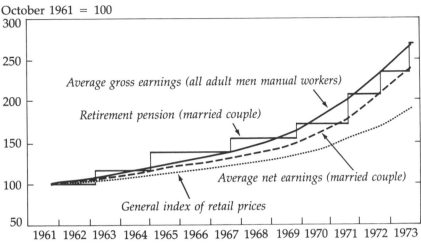

October 1961 = 100

Average gross earnings (all adult men manual workers)

Retirement pension (married couple)

Average net earnings (married couple)

General index of retail prices

1961 1962 1963 1964 1965 1966 1967 1968 1969 1970 1971 1972 1973

SOURCE: Government Statistical Service, *Social Trends*, No. 5, 1974 (London: HMSO, 1974).

manual worker and were substantially above the general increase in retail prices.

The first attempt at a more formal method of dealing with inflation was made in 1971. Legislation was enacted requiring an annual review of pension benefits for the purpose of rectifying the effects of inflation. As figure 1 shows, since 1971 pension increases have been roughly equal to the increase in the average wage over the preceding year. The Social Security Act of 1973, passed by the Conservative government, provided for a method of annual increases in pensions called *upratings*, based on changes in prices.

No upratings actually occurred under this act, however. In the following year, there was a change of government, and the Labour party passed the National Insurance Act of 1974. Under that act, the annual upratings were required to be based on average earnings rather than prices, should wage indexing prove more beneficial to pensioners.[27]

Under the 1974 act, the secretary of state for social services is required to make an annual review of pension benefits to determine

---

[27] By 1974, annual increases in the average wage in Britain had exceeded annual increases in the general level of prices in every year since 1945.

whether they have "retained their value in relation to the general level of earnings or prices."[28] The choice between earnings and prices was to be made by choosing the one that showed the highest rate of increase. If the secretary concluded that no increase in pension benefits was required, he was to "lay before each House of Parliament a report explaining his reasons for arriving at that determination." On the other hand, if the secretary found that pension benefits had not retained their value, he was required to make an order increasing benefits "at least to such extent as he thinks necessary to restore their value."

The secretary was given a considerable amount of discretion in deciding how to measure changes in the level of earnings or prices. He also had the option of increasing pension benefits more frequently than once a year. During the rapid inflation from 1974 to 1978, upratings were made at six-month intervals on several occasions.

The law requires that an order increasing benefits, or a report explaining why no increase was necessary, be accompanied by a report by the government actuary. The actuary's report deals with the effects of increasing or not increasing benefits on the National Insurance Fund.

When the new pension system was initiated in April 1978, the flat-rate pension was to be increased on the basis of the more favorable choice of earnings or prices. The Conservative government, however, has recently changed this provision, and it now appears that the flat-rate pension will be price indexed.

The treatment of the earnings-related pension is slightly different and is a result of a compromise between the Labour party's traditional preference for wage indexing and the Conservative party's preference for price indexing. The worker's salary, on which the earnings-related pension is paid, will be revalued annually in line with the general increase in earnings up to the point of retirement. When he retires, however, the pension will be increased annually in line with the increase in prices.

Consider a worker who has received annual salary increases exactly proportional to the general increase in wages over his working years and has a weekly salary of fifty pounds in the final year before retirement. His average preretirement salary would be fifty pounds, and pensionable earnings would be fifty pounds minus the lower earnings limit. Because his earnings in previous years, although less than fifty pounds, are revalued in line with the general increase in

---

[28] See E. A. Johnson, "The Effects of Inflation and Currency Instability on Pension Schemes in the United Kingdom," in *Pensions and Inflation*, p. 96.

earnings, his revalued salary would be fifty pounds for each year of employment. If the worker's salary had grown at a faster rate than the rate of increase in average wages, the average salary used for computing his pension would be less than his salary in the final year before retirement. Conversely, if the worker's salary had grown at a slower rate than the rate of increase in average wages, his pension would be based on an average salary in excess of his wage during his last year of employment.

A problem that arises with any indexing procedure is the problem of dealing with *lags* in the adjustment process, especially when rates of inflation are high. Figure 1 shows the "staircase" growth of the flat-rate pension compared with continuous growth of wages.

This difference in the appearance of the two lines is significant to the pensioner. At the beginning of 1965, pensioners received a big boost in benefit payments well in advance of the increase in wages. So substantial was the pension hike that it was not until the latter part of 1967 that wages caught up with the pension. At that point, there was another pension hike. In contrast, the pension hikes in 1971, 1972, and 1973 did nothing more than allow the pension to catch up with wage increases that had already occurred.

From the point of view of the pensioner, before is better than after. In 1965, pensioners got a boost in real income that was not dissipated by wage inflation until late in 1967. On the other hand, in the 1970s pension hikes only matched the wage inflation that had already occurred. In the intervening year, pensioners suffered a real income loss.

One way of looking at the magnitudes of these gains and losses is to picture the two growth lines as forming a series of triangles. In the 1960s the triangles appear above the wage line. In the early 1970s the triangles appear below the wage line. In general, a triangle formed above the wage line represents an income gain, and the larger the area of the triangle, the larger the gain. Triangles formed below the wage line represent income losses, and the larger area of the triangle, the larger the loss.

The method of indexing used during the 1970s tends to penalize the pensioner. At very high rates of inflation, the triangles are larger, tending to increase the size of the penalty. Although one way to counteract this effect is by making more frequent upratings, a number of administrative obstacles stand in the way.

In practice, adjustments in pension benefits were based on published wage indexes, and these indexes were generally published three months after the month to which they relate. On top of this, another five months was usually required to put the benefit increase into effect. Thus, on the average, at least an eight-month lag can be expected between the month during which a wage increase occurs and the month during which a resulting pension hike is put into effect.[29]

As a result of these problems, an alternative procedure was put into effect. The social services secretary is now required to base upratings on projected rates of inflation. During periods of high and variable rates of inflation, however, such predictions—even for only eight months in advance—could be wide of the mark.

The Earnings Rule

The social security systems in both Britain and the United States pay full benefits only if a worker satisfies a *retirement test*.[30] The retirement test is theoretically defended on the following grounds: Retirement pensions are designed to provide a minimum income for those who are no longer employed. Because the pension is designed to replace part of the income the worker would have earned had he remained in employment, there is no reason to pay a pension to a worker who continues working.

Both the British and American systems have allowed workers to earn a limited amount of income and still qualify for a full pension. Moreover, above the limited amount, workers are allowed to earn additional income with only a partial sacrifice of the pension. In England, this set of restrictions is called the *earnings rule*.

The British system is more liberal than the American system in terms of the amount of income retirees may earn and still qualify for a full pension. In Britain, the amount of earnings exempt from the earnings rule is about 50 percent of the average wage paid in manufacturing. In the United States, the amount of earnings exempt is between 35 and 40 percent of the average wage. For workers who earn more than this limit, however, the British earnings rule is much tougher than in the United States. Although a British worker could earn up to £35 a week in 1976 and still receive a full pension, on earnings between £35 and £39 his retirement pension was reduced £0.5 for each £1 of earnings, and on all earnings above £39 his pension was reduced by an amount equal to additional earnings. Unlike the

---

[29] See ibid., pp. 102-103.

[30] A survey of the social security systems in more than 100 countries found that more than 80 percent of them have a retirement test. Underdeveloped countries tend to require total withdrawal from the labor force, whereas most developed countries permit some limited amount of earnings. See Elizabeth K. Kirkpatrick, "The Retirement Test: An International Study," *Social Security Bulletin*, July 1974, pp. 3–16.

current retirement test in the United States, the British test does not ask the worker to continue to sacrifice £0.5 of pension for each £1 of earnings until the pension is exhausted. As in the United States, the worker in Britain pays income and social security taxes on the income he earns. Since the total social security tax rate was 14.5 percent in 1976, the British worker faced a tax rate of 64.5 percent on each £1 of earnings between £35 and £39, not including income taxes. In addition, with a basic pension of £15.30, a British worker sacrificed his total pension at a weekly wage of £52.30.[31] If the British worker had been subject to the same effective tax rates as in the United States, his entire pension would not have been exhausted until the weekly wage reached £61.30.

The harsher treatment in Britain is partly ameliorated by giving persons who defer retirement beyond the eligibility age an increase in their pensions at retirement equal to one-seventh of 1 percent for every week that retirement is deferred, up to five years of deferment. Eight weeks of deferral must take place before a worker is entitled to such an increase.

The financial incentives for persons to work beyond the eligibility age are still quite weak. If a worker defers his retirement for the full five years, his pension is increased by about 37 percent. He would have to live more than eighteen years beyond the eligibility age to recoup the amount of his lost pension during the five years of deferral—to say nothing of the time value of money.

As in the United States, once a worker reaches a certain age, the earnings rule is discarded. All male workers seventy years of age or older are treated as retired, regardless of income. In contrast to the policy in the United States, persons seventy years of age and older are no longer liable for the employee's share of social security taxes. (The employer's share is not exempted.)[32]

At the time the new pension system was proposed, the earnings rule came under sharp attack by the Conservative party and some members of the Labour party. The government defended the earnings rule by arguing that its abolition would cost the government £85 million. The Conservatives argued that abolition of the rule would result in greater output, and because of additional production,

[31] On the first £4 of earnings over £35, the worker sacrifices £2 of pension. The remaining £13.70 are sacrificed on a pound-for-pound basis, so the total pension is exhausted at £52.30 (£39 + £13.30).

[32] All pensioners aged eighty and over are also paid an additional weekly pension. In 1977, this additional pension amounted to £0.25 per week. Also, a noncontributory pension is paid to all persons aged eighty and over who do not otherwise qualify for a regular pension.

37

the government would recoup some of its lost revenue. The Conservatives estimated the cost of abolishing the earnings rule at only £4 million—a small price to pay for the larger gross national product (GNP) and the greater freedom of choice and financial security for the elderly.[33]

A compromise between the Conservative and Labour parties on the earnings rule was made in the new system. Although the earnings rule is retained, the earnings limits established under the rule will be indexed along with the flat-rate pension. In addition, the earnings rule now applies only to the flat-rate pension. The earnings-related pension is not reduced if a worker continues working past the eligibility age.[34] With the passage of time, the earnings-related pension will comprise a larger and larger proportion of the average worker's total pension. Because the flat-rate portion of the total pension decreases as income increases, however, the economic effect of the new earnings rule is highly regressive.[35]

The Problem of Funding Future Pensions

The British social security system operates on a pay-as-you-go basis. Payroll tax revenues are paid out almost immediately in social security benefits. It was not always intended to be so. Lord Beveridge had wanted pensions to be "genuinely contributory." This would have required the buildup of a substantial fund.[36]

The buildup never occurred. As table 8 shows, since the beginning of the Beveridge plan in 1948, benefit increases have exhausted most of the payroll tax dollars collected. In 1948, the National Insurance Fund was only large enough to continue paying benefits for the next two years and eight months. By 1971, that period had been reduced to four months.[37]

[33] The Conservative argument was presented in a document by Kenneth Clark and Christopher Mockler, *An End to the Earnings Rule* (London: Conservative Political Center, 1976).

[34] Part of the rationale for this change was based on the fact that private pensions in Britain have no earnings rule. As a result, it was argued that workers fully participating in the state system should not face greater burdens than workers participating in contracted-out pension plans. See "Government Launches New Pension Scheme," p. 7.

[35] The flat-rate pension of a worker earning the maximum earnings limit is about one-seventh of preretirement earnings. For workers earning up to the lower earnings limit, the flat-rate pension is 100 percent of earnings. After the system reaches maturity, the flat-rate pension will be about 36 percent of the total pension for a worker earning the maximum earnings limit.

[36] See Arthur Seldon, *The Great Pension "Swindle"* (London: Tom Stacey, 1970), p. 58ff.

[37] A comparable situation exists in the United States. The Old Age Survivors Insurance trust fund had sufficient resources to pay benefits for one year and two months in

TABLE 8

NATIONAL INSURANCE (RESERVE) FUND, SELECTED YEARS, 1948–1971
(in billions of pounds)

End of Year	Total Amount of Fund[a]	Annual Expenditures for National Insurance
1948	0.8	0.3
1952	0.8	0.5
1953	1.1	0.5
1955	1.1	0.6
1956	1.2	0.7
1968	1.2	2.1
1969	0.9	2.3
1970	0.9	2.5
1971	0.9	2.6

[a] The size of the fund was unchanged during 1948–1952, 1953–1955, and 1956–1968.
SOURCE: Leif Haans-Olsen, "Social Security Funding Practices in Selected Countries," *Social Security Bulletin*, May 1976, p. 5.

The National Insurance Fund covers a great many social welfare programs—health, work injury, unemployment, invalidism, and survivors' insurance—in addition to retirement pensions. About two-thirds of annual expenditures are in the form of retirement pensions. If the 18 percent treasury supplement to the fund is assumed to be allocated to other programs, an estimated 82 percent of payroll taxes would go to retirement pensions each year.

The social security system in Britain faces the same type of funding problem as that in other industrialized countries. Because it is a pay-as-you-go system, the ability to pay benefits depends crucially on the number of taxpayers relative to the number of beneficiaries. If the number of beneficiaries grows, relative to the number of taxpayers, tax rates must be increased in order to maintain existing levels of benefit.

In Britain, higher and higher tax rates have been required in order to maintain the real (wage-indexed) value of pension benefits. Table 9 shows part of the reason. In 1931, the ratio of the number of persons aged sixty-five and over to those aged fifteen to sixty-four was less than 11 percent. Thirty years later, in 1961, that ratio had increased to 18 percent.

1970 and only eight months in 1975. See Leif Haanes-Olsen, "Social Security Funding Practices in Selected Countries," *Social Security Bulletin*, May 1976, pp. 1–6.

TABLE 9

POPULATION TRENDS IN GREAT BRITAIN, 1861–1971
(population in millions)

Census Year	Persons Aged 15 to 64	Persons Aged 65 and Over	Ratio of Persons 65 and Over to Age 15 to 64 (%)
1861	13.8	1.1	8
1871	15.4	1.2	8
1881	17.5	1.4	8
1891	19.8	1.6	8
1901	23.2	1.7	7
1911	26.1	2.1	8
1921	28.2	2.6	9
1931	30.7	3.3	10
1941	—	—	—
1951	32.6	5.3	16
1961	33.3	6.0	18
1971	33.9	7.1	21

SOURCE: Central Statistical Office, *Annual Abstract of Statistics* (London: HMSO, selected years).

What is more, if current population trends continue, the ratio of retired persons to persons of working age will increase. A stable rate of population growth is necessary in order to keep a constant ratio of beneficiaries to workers. A falling rate of population growth causes this ratio to rise. As shown in table 10, from 1960 to 1974, the rate of growth of the British population has steadily declined—from about 0.8 percent per year in 1960 to 0.1 percent per year in 1974.

The reports of the government actuary in Britain predict that the portion of the population of pensionable age will reach a high in the late 1970s and will then begin a steady decline until 2011. As shown in table 11, the ratio of males sixty-five and older to the male population of working age will reach a peak of 17.8 percent by 1981 and is expected to fall to 16.5 percent by the year 2011. The serious long-run financing problem will start about a decade after 2011. At that time, there will be a sharp drop in the size of the working population because of the decline in the rate of growth of the population shown in table 10. Because of this demographic change, the ratio of retired persons to workers will rise, and payroll tax rates will have to be increased.

A comparison of tables 9 and 11 shows that the British are faced

TABLE 10

ANNUAL RATE OF GROWTH OF POPULATION, UNITED KINGDOM, 1960–1974
(percent)

Census Year	Growth Rate
1960	0.8
1961	0.8
1962	0.5
1963	0.6
1964	0.6
1965	0.6
1966	0.5
1967	0.5
1968	0.4
1969	0.3
1970	0.3
1971	0.3
1972	0.2
1973	0.1
1974	0.1

NOTE: Growth rate = birth rate minus death rate.
SOURCE: Bureau of the Census, *World Population, 1975* (Washington, D.C.: U.S. Dept. of Commerce, 1976), p. 209.

with a special problem. Since the eligibility age is sixty for women, and since more and more women are entering the labor force, in the future the number of women drawing pensions will increase. When women age sixty through sixty-four are included as pensionable in the dependence ratio, the ratio jumps from 16 to 21.2 percent in 1951 and from 18 to 23.6 percent in 1961, although in these years most of the women over age sixty were not drawing pensions in their own right. In the future, when a great many more of them will be, the burden of taxation faced by succeeding generations will tend to increase.[38]

Another phenomenon creating funding problems in Britain is early retirement. In Britain today, 26 percent of all private pension programs establish sixty as the normal pensionable age. Most civil servants can retire at age sixty, and policemen, after thirty years of service, can retire at age fifty. In addition, more and more union members are choosing early retirement.

[38] See Johnson, "Effects of Inflation and Currency Instability," pp. 105–106.

41

TABLE 11

POPULATION OVER PENSIONABLE AGE COMPARED WITH POPULATION BETWEEN AGE FIFTEEN AND THE PENSIONABLE AGE, UNITED KINGDOM, 1951–2011

(percent)

Year	Males	Females	Male and Female
1951	13.8	28.9	21.2
1961	14.0	33.8	23.6
1971	16.2	39.5	27.3
1976	17.5	40.8	28.6
1981	17.8	40.2	28.4
1991	17.8	39.3	28.0
2001	16.7	35.9	25.9
2011	16.5	36.9	26.2

NOTE: Pensionable age for males is sixty-five; for females, sixty.
SOURCE: E. A. Johnson (the government actuary), "The Effects of Inflation and Currency Instability on Pension Schemes in the United Kingdom," in *Pensions and Inflation* (Geneva: International Labor Office, 1977), p. 105.

Although male retirees are not able to draw social security pensions until they reach age sixty-five, if they choose to retire early and live on their private pensions or civil service pensions, they will not be working and paying taxes to support the social security system. The trend toward early retirement also puts political pressure on the government to lower the age of eligibility for social security.

The existence of high and variable rates of inflation also contributes to short-run funding problems. With indexing, total benefit payments rise with the rate of inflation and with the frequency of upratings. There are also problems on the tax side, even though the payroll tax is proportionate to income and rises as wages rise.

The maximum tax payable is calculated on the basis of the upper earnings limit, and between upratings this limit remains constant. Because adjustments to inflation are not made immediately, as the rate of inflation changes, substantial surpluses or deficits can occur, depending on the exact timing of the increases in contribution ceilings as well as increases in benefits.[39]

The funding problems generated by inflation, however, tend to be temporary. Over the long run, a pay-as-you-go system has an important advantage under conditions of inflation—although indexed benefits must be increased, tax receipts increase automatically as wages rise.

[39] See ibid., p. 102.

3

Contracting Out

The most interesting aspect of the British social security system is the provision for contracting out. Employers with private pension plans (occupational pension schemes) are now able to contract their employees out of the earnings-related component of the social security system.

The Basic Requirements for Contracting Out

Certain conditions are necessary for contracting out. In general employees covered by private pension plans may not be contracted out unless the plan promises benefits at least equal to the benefits promised by the earnings-related component of the national system. The specific requirements for contracting out are:

1. The private pension plan must be based on final salary or average salary revalued in line with the growth of national average earnings.

2. The private pension plan must provide the employee with a *requisite benefit*—an annual pension equal to 1.25 percent (one-eightieth) of average earnings for each year of contracted-out employment. Overtime or bonus pay may be excluded from an employee's total earnings. In addition, the plan may exclude income above the maximum earnings limit or an amount up to one-and-one-half times the lower earnings limit. In all cases, however, requirement 3 must be satisfied.

3. The private plan must provide each covered employee with a *guaranteed minimum pension* (GMP) that is at least equal to the amount of the earnings-related pension he would have earned in that employment had he not been contracted out.[1] In other words, it must

---

[1] There is an exception to this condition. According to the twenty-best-years rule, after twenty years of operation, the earnings-related component of the new pension system is calculated on the basis of earnings in the twenty best years of employment. These twenty years need not be the last twenty. Nor do they need to be consecutive. Private pensions are not subject to the twenty-best-years rule. If the rule would generate an extra private pension for the employee, this extra pension is provided by the government.

provide a pension equal to 1.25 percent of salary between the earnings limits for each year of contracted-out employment.[2] After twenty years of contracting out, the pension of each employee will be equal to 25 percent of his pensionable salary.

4. The pension must be available at the official eligibility age (sixty-five for men and sixty for women).

5. The guaranteed minimum pension must be increased by one-seventh of 1 percent a week if a covered employee postpones retirement beyond the eligibility age.

6. A widow's guaranteed minimum pension must be at least one-half her husband's, with the remainder being paid by the government. If a deceased husband's requisite benefit exceeds his guaranteed minimum pension, the widow is entitled to one-half the requisite benefit. This, unlike the GMP, may be paid as a lump sum if the husband dies before retirement. The government is not obliged to make up the other half of the requisite benefit.

7. Each private plan must have a contracting-out certificate issued by the Occupational Pensions Board approving the contracting-out conditions of the plan.

The Option

The option to contract out raises the question: Under what conditions can employees expect to benefit by contracting out? If a private fund promises pension benefits identical to those promised by the government, the relevant question is one of cost. Could private pension funds offer benefits identical to those promised by the government at a lower cost? The same question may be expressed another way: Would workers fare better under the national insurance system than they would if they invested those same tax dollars in the private securities market?

To answer this question, suppose the British government had adopted a truly voluntary scheme, giving each worker the option of either paying additional social security taxes to the government or investing a comparable sum in a private investment fund. A fundamental characteristic of social security systems funded on a pay-as-you-go basis is that *in a mature system with a stable population, social*

---

[2] If the private plan does not base its pension on total earnings, it is possible for the GMP to exceed the requisite benefit. In all cases, the private plan must pay the higher of the two types of benefits.

security can at most pay the average worker a rate of return equal to the rate of growth of average wages.[3]

If the population is stable, the ratio of the number of beneficiaries to the number of workers will be constant. If the system is mature, all covered persons will pay the same tax rate over their working lives. Under such conditions, if benefits are increased in proportion to average covered wages, workers will receive a rate of return equal to the rate of growth of average covered wages. The rate of return received by persons paying social security taxes would be expected to be no more than 2 or 3 percent—the real rate of growth of average wages in most industrialized countries. In contrast, rates of return on equity have usually been three to four times this amount—generally in the neighborhood of 8 to 10 percent.[4]

Under such conditions, participation in social security would be a relatively bad investment. Workers would receive a rate of return below the rate of return they could have earned by investing in a portfolio of common stocks. It would not be to the advantage of every worker to opt out of the social security system, however, because past taxes are sunk costs. For persons nearing the retirement age, it would be advantageous to pay social security taxes for a few more years in return for additional benefits. Nonetheless, for most young workers it would be advantageous to opt out of the system.

The Problem of Voluntary Social Security. If the private pension market can offer a better deal than social security to most young workers but not to older workers, contracting out faces a major problem. If the decision to opt out were left to the individual worker, a voluntary system would produce the following scenario: The majority of young workers, after discovering that private securities promise a higher rate of return, would choose to opt out. As a result, the number of taxpayers would decrease while the number of beneficiaries remained unchanged. Since the system is financed on a pay-as-you-go basis, taxes paid by workers remaining in the system would have to be raised in order to meet current obligations. The increase in tax rates would induce still more workers to leave the system. Taxes would then have to be raised again. A merry-go-round of higher and higher tax rates and fewer and fewer taxpayers would

[3] See, for example, Martin Feldstein, "Facing the Social Security Crisis," *Public Interest*, Spring 1977, p. 92.
[4] Roger G. Ibbotson and Rex A. Sinquefield, "Stocks, Bonds, Bills and Inflation: Year-by-Year Historical Returns (1926–1974)," *Journal of Business*, vol. 49 (January 1976).

thus ensue. Eventually the system would be left with only beneficiaries. No one would volunteer to be a taxpayer.

Restrictions on Contracting Out

To prevent a mass withdrawal of persons paying taxes, the British
system has imposed two principal restrictions on contracting out:

1. Only persons covered by approved private pension plans may
be contracted out.

2. In electing to contract out, the employer may not differentiate
between employees on any ground other than the nature of their
employment.

Because of the first restriction, a worker may not opt out on his
own. Under the second restriction, employers are not allowed to
contract out only male blue-collar workers or only those of certain
ages. In addition, all must be contracted out on the same terms—
all must pay at the same contribution rates and all receive the same
benefits.[5]

These two restrictions put a brake on the potential exodus of
young male workers. Pensions cannot be sold like life insurance
policies by giving favorable rates to favorably situated individuals.
They can only be sold to entire groups of people—groups that include
young and old, male and female. In addition, a private pension fund
beginning in 1978 and promising benefits identical to those promised
by the government can afford to pay such benefits to older workers,
especially older female workers, only by subsidizing these benefits
with contributions from younger workers, especially younger male
workers.

The new social security system initially offers a better deal to
older workers than it does to younger workers. It also offers a better
deal to some female workers than it does to male workers. Such
redistributions would be unlikely to occur in the private pension

---

[5] These restrictions apply only to the requisite (and guaranteed minimum pension)
level of benefits. They do not apply to additional benefits. Nor do they appear to
apply to private plans that are not contracted out. See *The Castle Scheme and Its Effect
on the Design of Occupational Pensions* (London: Metropolitan Pensions Association,
1975), p. 21. In addition, contracted-out plans are entitled to exclude those workers
who are within five years of retirement (see Max Horlick and Alfred Skolnik, "Man-
dating Private Pensions: A Four Country Study," unpublished, Office of Research
and Statistics, Social Security Administration, Washington, D.C., February 28, 1978).

Quite apart from the conditions for contracting out, private pensions are still
governed by the doctrine of "equal access." The law requires systems that impose
conditions on entry, such as a certain length of service, to do so in a way that does
not discriminate between men and women.

market. In the private pension market, each worker tends to be paid the same rate of return. The restrictions on contracting out, however, hamper the ability of private pension plans to do this. In effect, pension funds are forced by government to redistribute wealth among their members in the same way that the social security system redistributes wealth.[6]

Of course, not all private pension plans are alike. Some contain a higher proportion of young workers than others. Some contain a higher proportion of male workers than others. Nonetheless, the effect of the two restrictions is to dampen the incentive of employees to contract out.

If private pension funds are forced to provide benefits identical to those promised by the social security system, the projected cost of providing guaranteed minimum pensions would be higher for the private funds than for the government, and the private pension funds would have to charge a higher premium than the premium charged by the government. This is because *private pension funds are required to build up a fund, whereas the social security system is not.* It has been estimated that the private pension fund would have to charge an average premium of about 7 percent compared with the very low government premium that would grow over time to only 5 percent.

Guaranteed Minimum Benefits Must Be Guaranteed. A third restriction included in the new system is that guaranteed minimum pension benefits must be guaranteed. This was initially viewed by employers with great alarm. At first glance, this restriction does not seem unduly burdensome. After all, insurance companies regularly make guarantees about the amounts they will pay if uncertain events occur. Also, banks and corporate borrowers often promise to pay fixed interest payments to lenders, even though future market rates of interest as well as future profits are uncertain.

The difficulty to employers stems largely from the unpredictable effects of inflation. With inflation, there is no limit to an employer's pension obligations. This is because the guaranteed pension is a percentage of an employee's wages, and under inflationary conditions there is no limit to how high wages can rise. With inflation, a pension fund would also earn high nominal rates of return on its investments. The effects of inflation on rates of return are extremely uncertain, however.

---

[6] Actually, such redistribution need not occur in some already established private pension plans. This is because most plans already provide benefits well in excess of the guaranteed minimum pension required by the new pension scheme (see ch. 4).

The way in which inflation may affect capital markets is illustrated by the way British investors have fared over the past several decades. From 1952 to 1962, the annual real rate of return earned by holding a random selection of British common stocks was 10.9 percent. For the decade beginning in 1956, the real rate of return was 9.4 percent. The corresponding figure for 1961 was 3.8 percent, and for 1965 it dropped to 0.6 percent.[7] Although more recent figures are not available, it appears that in comparison with the high rates of return in earlier decades, the real rate of return for the 1970s—a period of very rapid inflation—may be negative. In addition, the real rate of return on corporate bonds has been below the return on equities.

Experience in Britain during the past decade suggests that the higher the rate of inflation and the more volatile the rate of inflation, the lower the yield that capital markets generate. Although in the past the rate of return on equities has been substantially higher than the rate of growth of real wages, no one can be certain that the rate of growth of real wages will not exceed the real return on capital in the future.

The requirement that employers who contract out guarantee their pension benefits was included in the white paper, "Better Pensions," published in September 1974.[8] At that time, a majority of pension advisers concluded that this condition was impossible for employers to accept, and it looked as though few employers would be willing to contract out.[9]

To avoid the possibility that very few workers would be contracted out, the new system was altered in two ways. First, the reduction in the employees' payroll tax rate for those contracting out was raised to a level of 7 percent in the initial years. Second, a

[7] See E. A. Johnson, "The Effects of Inflation and Currency Instability on Pension Schemes in the United Kingdom," in *Pensions and Inflation* (Geneva: International Labor Office, 1977), pp. 104–105.

[8] In the past, most private pension fund agreements permitted the employer to discontinue the fund if the assets of the fund were not sufficient to cover promised benefits. If the fund had assets equal to 80 percent of promised benefits at the date of discontinuance, for example, each employee would receive 80 percent of his projected benefit rather than the full benefit. This option to discontinue still applies to benefits in excess of the GMP benefits.

[9] The reluctance of employers to guarantee benefits is not surprising. One of the reasons why common stocks typically pay a higher rate of return than fixed-interest securities is that the return on stocks is not guaranteed. The only way a typical employee can hope to earn a higher real rate of return in the private capital market than he can earn on his social security tax payments is by accepting some risk. The behavior of the private pension market suggests that employees are willing to do so, however.

method was devised to allow employers to limit their liability under contracting out—ultimately, the burden of guaranteeing benefits was shifted to the government.

Payroll Taxes for Contracted-Out Employees

Under the new pension system, employees who are contracted out of the earnings-related component pay the following tax rates on weekly earnings, starting in April 1978:

- on earnings up to the minimum earnings limit:

Employee tax rate	6.5%
Employer tax rate	12.0
Total tax rate	18.5

- on earnings above the minimum earnings limit and up to the maximum earnings limit:

Employee tax rate	4.0%
Employer tax rate	7.5
Total tax rate	11.5

On earnings up to the minimum earnings limit, contracted-out employees pay the same 18.5 percent payroll tax rate as that paid by employees who are not contracted out. On income between the earnings limits (and including the upper earnings limit), however, they pay a tax rate 7 percent lower than that paid by workers who do not opt out. The employee's tax rate is reduced by 2.5 percentage points, and the employer's tax rate is reduced by 4.5 percentage points.

A curious result of this tax structure is that workers who are contracted out pay payroll taxes that are regressive with respect to income. A contracted-out employee earning only the minimum earnings limit must pay taxes equal to 18.5 percent of income. In contrast, a contracted-out employee earning the maximum earnings limit pays taxes equal to approximately 13.0 percent of income when the tax on earnings up to the minimum earnings limit is added to the tax on earnings between the minimum and maximum earnings limits. Upon retirement, both workers will receive the same amount in benefits from the government.

The tax rate on the second tier of earnings is intended to encourage contracting out. For income between the two earnings limits, the abatement rate, or reduction in the tax rate offered to those who contract out, is 7 percent. This abatement rate is intended to apply only for the first five years, however. It will then be reduced by half of 1 percent every five years until the new pension system reaches maturity. After twenty years, the abatement rate will be 5 percent.[10]

In the start-up period, the 7 percent abatement rate increases to employers the attractiveness of contracting out. The variations in the cost to private pensions of providing the guaranteed minimum pension is shown by age and sex in figure 2. The "cost" is equal to the number of pounds of each £100 of earnings—or the percentage of the worker's salary—that is required by a private pension in order to pay the guaranteed minimum pension. The cost of providing the guaranteed minimum pension rises dramatically with age. For a male worker at the age of twenty-five, the guaranteed minimum pension can be purchased for a premium equal to about 3 percent of his salary; for a fifty-eight-year-old male worker, the cost amounts to about 9 percent of his salary.

The line in figure 2 intersecting the vertical axis at five pounds (5 percent of salary) represents the government's estimate of the "cost" of providing the earnings-related pension when the system reaches maturity. It is also the proposed *abatement rate* for the system at maturity—the reduction in the payroll tax rate promised to employees who contract out.

Figure 2 can be roughly interpreted in the following way: At age levels at which the cost of providing the GMP for each £100 of earnings is less than £5, workers would gain by contracting out; at age levels at which the cost of providing the GMP for each £100 of earnings is greater than £5, workers would gain by remaining in the system. According to this figure, all male workers below the age of thirty-eight and all female workers below the age of twenty-seven and a half would gain by opting out. In contrast, all older workers would gain by remaining in the system. The assumptions underlying the proposed abatement rate are probably too conservative. If capital markets in the future perform as in the past, the yield on private pension plans should exceed the rate of growth of average wages by more than 1 percent (the assumption used in figure 2).

An abatement rate of 7 percent is identical to the government actuary's estimate of the cost of providing contracted-out benefits to the entire population. This probably accounts for the choice of 7 percent. The effective abatement rate, however, is higher than 7 percent.

British tax law, like the American tax law, requires employees to pay income taxes on the share of the payroll tax nominally allocated to them. When a contribution to a private pension fund is

[10] This is the current projection (see *The Castle Scheme and Its Effect on the Design of Occupational Pensions,* p. 22).

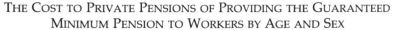

FIGURE 2
THE COST TO PRIVATE PENSIONS OF PROVIDING THE GUARANTEED
MINIMUM PENSION TO WORKERS BY AGE AND SEX

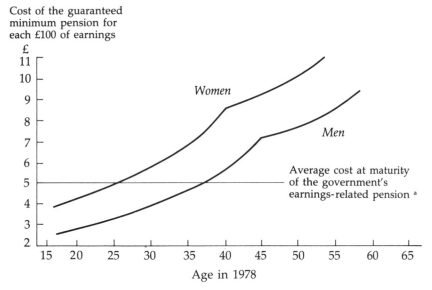

Cost of the guaranteed
minimum pension for
each £100 of earnings

Average cost at maturity
of the government's
earnings-related pension [a]

Age in 1978

[a] The cost at maturity (£5 for each £100 of earnings) is based on a 9 percent long-term rate of interest and an 8 percent rate of growth of earnings (a differential of 1 percent). Assumptions about expected mortality, by age and sex, are those of the government actuary.

SOURCE: Reproduced from *The Castle Scheme and Its Effect on the Design of Occupational Pensions,* with the permission of the Metropolitan Pensions Association, London.

made by an employer, however, the employee realizes a tax advantage. The Metropolitan Pensions Association in Britain calculates that when these tax advantages are included, the effective reduction in the tax rate for the average employee contracted out is about 8.35 percent.[11] Moreover, at this rate, the critical ages rise to fifty for men and forty for women.

Inflation-Proofing

The earnings-related component of the new state pension system involves wage indexing of the pension at retirement and price indexing during retirement years. These indexing provisions are required for all employees, whether or not they are contracted out.

If employers cease contracting out, the guaranteed minimum

[11] Ibid., p. 23.

pension of employees built up during the period of contracting out must be fully secured. In fact, before a contracting-out certificate can be granted to an employer, he must show exactly how he intends to secure the guaranteed minimum pensions and their annual revaluation in the event that his employees cease to be contracted out.

Employers appeared unwilling to guarantee indexed benefits in the way proposed in the original white paper because of the open-ended liabilities such a policy would create. In the new law, the government has allowed employers to limit their liability in two important ways. First, the government has assumed the obligation to inflation-proof the worker's guaranteed minimum pension once the worker retires. Second, the law allows the employer to limit his liability to the employee before retirement by providing the employer with a series of options.

There are three types of circumstances under which an employer might desire to limit his liability:

1. A worker might terminate employment within five years of being contracted out but before reaching retirement age.

2. A worker might terminate employment after five years of being contracted out but before reaching retirement age.

3. The total membership, including pensioners, of a contracted-out pension plan might cease to be contracted out.

In all three cases, employers have the option to retain their obligation to provide the guaranteed minimum pensions and revalue them each year.[12] Such an option might be preferred if the performance of capital markets is such that the guaranteed minimum pension remains fully secured. A serious problem arises when the assets of the fund fall short of promised benefits. In that event, the employer is potentially liable for the balance of the shortfall. A less serious problem arises when the employer simply wants to end his obligations under the plan, even though the fund is fully secured.

Under the new law, employers contracting out can calculate what their maximum liability will be if they desire to end their obligations under the plan. In case 1 above, when an employee leaves contracted-out employment *within five years*, his guaranteed minimum pension may be secured by shifting the obligation back to the government.[13] This may be accomplished through the payment of a *contributions equivalent premium* (CEP)—the difference between the

[12] In case 1, exercise of this option requires the employee's consent.
[13] During the initial five years under the new pension system, some workers who terminate employment within five years may have acquired preserved pension rights and are treated as though they had five years or more of contracted-out employment.

total amount of social security taxes that would have been paid had the employee not been contracted out and the amount of the taxes that were actually paid.[14]

In case 2, all employees with five or more years of contracted-out employment qualify for *preserved* pension rights. The employer may limit his revaluation liability for employees in this category to a maximum of a 5 percent increase per year in the amount owed the employee through the payment of a *limited revaluation premium* (LRP)—the balance being guaranteed by the government. If, after paying the premium, the employer finds that required revaluation is only a 4 percent increase in the amount owed the employee, his liability will be 4 percent.

An employer may also limit his revaluation liability by an agreement to pay a *fixed* rate of revaluation, an increase of 8½ percent per year in the amount owed the employee. If the actual revaluation rate is 10½ percent, the government pays the additional 2 percent. On the other hand, if the actual revaluation rate is only 6½ percent, the government realizes a profit of 2 percent.

In case 3, the employer may choose to handle the guaranteed minimum pensions in the same manner as he would for individual withdrawals from service after five years of employment. That is, he may pay the limited revaluation premiums and restrict his obligation to a maximum increase of 5 percent a year in the amount owed the employee. Or he may elect to revalue the guaranteed minimum pensions at a fixed rate of 8½ percent per annum.

Alternatively, the employer may transfer the whole liability for guaranteed minimum premiums and their future revaluation back to the government. This option may involve the payment of two types of premiums.[15] For all employees who have not yet retired, the premium will be an *accrued rights premium* (ARP). For all employees who have retired, the premium will be a *pensioner's rights premium* (PRP).[16]

---

[14] Provisions also exist for transferring guaranteed minimum pensions to other contracted-out plans when workers change jobs.

[15] The amount of these premiums may vary from year to year or even from month to month. This is because the premiums themselves will be indexed in one of two ways. They may be indexed to the rate of growth of real wages, or they may be indexed by means of an *investment index*. An investment index would protect employers who withdraw from a contracted-out system from adverse market conditions at the time of termination. This index would be based on the yield of a hypothetical portfolio consisting of a random selection of common stocks (65 percent) and a random selection of fixed-interest securities (35 percent). In general, premiums charged by the state under this method of indexing will vary positively with variations in the index.

[16] Pensioner's rights premiums will probably be rare. For most retirees with pensions, an annuity will have been set up and paid for. Because inflation-proofing at this stage

In all cases, the premiums charged will reflect the actuarial liabilities given by the composition of the work force under the private pension plan. That is, unlike the payroll tax rates charged ordinary wage earners and salaried employees, the premiums charged firms who wish to limit their liability will reflect differences in age and sex of the employees.

When a contracted-out system is transferred back to the government, the accrued rights premiums applicable to employees who have yet to reach the retirement age will in part be paid by the employees themselves. In this case, the employees' share of the premium will normally be equal to the additional payroll tax the employee would have paid if he were fully participating in the full national pension system.

A final option, available to the employer who ceases to contract out, places even greater limits upon the employer's liabilities. This option, called the *12 percent option,* allows the employer to limit his obligations in retrospect. If the employer decides to cease contracting out, he may limit his obligation to revalue guaranteed minimum pensions in the five previous years to 12 percent per year. If revaluation has averaged 18 percent, for example, the employer will pay 12 percent and the government will pay the additional 6 percent.

In choosing the 12 percent option, the employer is not allowed to apply the rule selectively to particular years. It applies only to the average over the five-year period. In addition, the option only applies to employers who elect to pay ARP and PRP premiums. The option does not apply to employers who elect to retain guaranteed minimum pensions and revalue them themselves or to pay the fixed 8.5 percent revaluation.

These options significantly reduce an employer's potential liability. Unlike the original white paper proposal, current law is expected to give employers sufficient protection to encourage contracting out.

---

is the responsibility of the state, in order to take advantage of the right to pay such premiums the employer would have to surrender that part of the annuity representing the guaranteed minimum pension. It is unlikely that the employer would benefit by such a move.

4
Inducements to Contract Out

Currently, roughly half of all British workers are participating in private pension plans (see table 12). The bulk of these are probably contracted out. In 1971, when contracting out was first allowed, more than 72 percent of those in private pension plans were contracted out.[1] For workers who are contracted out, the government's earnings-related pension that they must give up is small compared with their private pension. In 1975, for example, private pension plans granted the average pensioner about 23 percent of his preretirement income.[2] The earnings-related pension amounts to only one-eightieth of salary between the earnings limits for each year of contracting-out service. A worker retiring one year after the new system began, for example, would receive an earnings-related social security pension equal to only 1.25 percent of his pensionable salary.

Over the next twenty years, the earnings-related pension will gradually increase to 25 percent of preretirement income. Many private pensions will still have an advantage because the replacement ratios that they provide will be larger than 25 percent. A typical private pension plan today promises one-sixtieth (1.66 percent) of preretirement income for each year of service.[3] Under such a plan, a worker who is employed for forty years would retire with a private pension equal to about 67 percent of preretirement income. Moreover, the percentages given for private pensions are based on total income. The earnings-related pension pertains only to income between the two earnings limits. If private pension benefits were taken as a percentage of income between the earnings limits only, the percentages would be much higher.[4]

[1] This is roughly 8 million employees. (See Martin B. Tracy, "Social Security Revision in the United Kingdom," *Social Security Bulletin*, November 1975, p. 33.)

[2] See Leif Haanes-Olsen, "Earnings-Replacement Rate of Old-Age Benefits, 1965–75, Selected Countries," *Social Security Bulletin*, January 1978, p. 14.

[3] Preretirement income is typically income in the last twelve months or the average of the highest three of the last ten years of service. In effect, private pension plans are implicitly wage indexed until the time of retirement.

[4] The higher the worker's salary, the greater will be the associated pension expressed as a percentage of income between the earnings limits.

TABLE 12

EMPLOYEES WITH PRIVATE PENSIONS, UNITED KINGDOM, 1971

Category of Worker	Total Number of Employees[a] (in millions)	Number of Employees with Pensions (in millions)	Pension Coverage (%)
White-collar			
Men	5.7	4.6	80.7
Women	4.0	1.8	45.0
Total	9.7	6.4	66.0
Blue-collar			
Men	8.0	4.1	51.3
Women	3.1	0.6	19.4
Total	11.1	4.7	23.6
Total	20.8	11.1	53.4

[a] Excludes employers who had no pension system for any of their staff. For purposes of comparison the total number of employed persons was 22.7 million.
SOURCE: Johnson, "Effects of Inflation and Currency Instability," p. 97.

Attractive Features

An Immediate Reduction in Payroll Tax Rates. The option to contract out makes possible an immediate reduction in payroll tax rates for most persons participating in private plans. Whereas they paid a total payroll tax of 16.5 percent of taxable income prior to April 1978, workers with earnings equal to the maximum earnings limit can now lower their payroll tax rate to approximately 13 percent.

An employee earning only the minimum earnings limit actually faces an increase in tax rates equal to 2 percent. On earnings up to the minimum earnings limit, the new tax rate is 18.5 percent. On the other hand, the tax rate on earnings between the minimum and maximum earnings limit is now only 11.5 percent for workers who contract out. For a worker with earnings equal to the maximum earnings limit, the 18.5 percent tax on earnings up to the minimum limit plus the 11.5 percent tax on earnings between the minimum and maximum limits yield a total payroll tax rate of approximately 13 percent. For workers with earnings below the maximum earnings limit, the total payroll tax rate will be higher than 13 percent, depending on the portion of their earnings subject to the 11.5 percent tax. Most members of private pension plans will probably get a tax reduction as a result of contracting out because they tend to earn relatively high incomes. Table 12 shows that 66 percent of white-collar workers are participating in private plans, compared with only 23.6 percent of blue-collar workers. White-collar workers have median incomes about one-sixth greater than those of manual workers and would be more likely to receive a tax reduction.[5] Also, persons with private pensions are disproportionately male, and male workers on the average have much higher incomes than women workers, enabling them to benefit from the tax reduction.

The value of the initial tax reduction will eventually be reduced. At maturity, the total payroll tax may well climb to 20 or 20.5 percent, and the abatement rate is scheduled to fall from 7 percent to 5 percent. At that time, the payroll tax rate paid by a contracted-out worker earning the maximum earnings limit will probably rise to 15 or 15.5 percent—not much lower than the 16.5 percent rate he paid prior to 1978. Indeed, because the government plans to add funds financed by general taxation to the National Insurance Fund, it is probably safe to assume that the worker will face increased tax rates generally. Ultimately, therefore, the contracted-out worker may be realizing no tax reduction at all.

Lower Tax Rates Than Those Paid by Fully Participating Workers. When the contracted-out worker is contrasted with a worker not contracted out, the position of the contracted-out worker looks even better. Under the new system, on earnings between the two earnings limits, the contracted-out worker initially faces a payroll tax rate that is seven percentage points lower than the rate faced by the fully participating worker. Even at maturity, the tax-rate differential will be 5 percent. The immediate effect of contracting out is that the contracted-out worker earning between the earnings limits may receive a substantial increase in his real income, whereas the fully participating worker does not.

There is, of course, another side to the coin. In return for a reduction in taxes, contracted-out workers give up the right to draw the government's earnings-related pension at retirement. There is still an inducement for young workers to opt out because the reduction in their taxes is larger than the value of their earnings-related pensions. As was shown in figure 2, when the system is mature, male workers below the age of thirty-eight and female workers below the age of twenty-seven and one-half would gain by opting out— the estimated cost of providing the guaranteed minimum benefit through private insurance is less than the five-percentage-point dif-

[5] Government Statistical Service, *Social Trends*, no. 5 (London: HMSO, 1974), p. 116.

ferential in the rate required of workers who fully participate. For workers nearing the retirement age, however, especially female workers, the earnings-related pension is usually worth more than the tax reduction. These workers will individually bear a loss from contracting out unless management and labor make certain adjustments in the private pension systems because of this possibility. Nonetheless, among contracted-out workers as a group, these possible losses must be balanced against the gains.

The loss of revenue because of the tax reductions on contracted-out workers must be made up by increasing taxes, either for workers who are not contracted out or for taxpayers generally, if the cost of contracting out is financed by general revenues. This is because contracting out does not immediately reduce the costs of a pay-as-you-go social security system. In a pay-as-you-go system, the total amount of revenue that must be collected depends on the cost of the benefits of those who are currently retired, and contracting out does not affect these costs. In April 1978, workers fully participating in the new system watched their payroll taxes rise two percentage points—from 16.5 percent of taxable income to 18.5 percent. The 2 percent higher payroll tax rate on participating workers was necessary in order to offset the payroll tax reduction enjoyed by workers who contracted out.

The labor market might redress the initial tax burden on fully participating workers if wages rose in industries where workers are predominantly participating in the national plan and wages fell for employment that is contracted out. Other things equal, young workers will prefer being contracted out to fully participating, and older workers will prefer fully participating to being contracted out. Undoubtedly, some wage adjustments will occur in order to make jobs offered by fully participating firms and contracted-out firms equally appealing to individuals seeking employment in the labor market.

If labor markets were perfectly competitive, in the long run the government would not be able to redistribute wealth among workers through its pension scheme. Wage adjustments would offset any differences in the value of pension plans. Still, conventional wisdom has it that British labor markets are perforated with pockets of monopoly power. It is where unions are strongest that private pension plans are likely to be flourishing. Some redistribution, therefore, will probably be unavoidable and will not be offset by labor market adjustments.[6]

[6] Some evidence that market wages reflect the discounted value of pension benefits is presented in Bradley Schiller and Randall Weiss, "Pensions and Wages: A Test for Equalizing Differences," unpublished, University of Maryland, January 1977.

Higher Rates of Return. The inducement to contract out depends significantly on how British workers fare under the new state pension system. As we have seen, the new pension system is a good deal for workers who retire during the start-up stage. For these workers, the value of additional taxes paid is generally less than the value of additional benefits they expect to receive. For the generation of workers entering the labor market today and for each succeeding generation, things look much worse. The return these workers can expect to receive on their social security taxes is quite low. For some, the return is even negative. Because of these low rates of return, there is a strong inducement for young workers to opt out of the system.

To estimate the rate of return that young workers will receive, the present (discounted) value of expected future benefits may be compared with the present value of expected future taxes (accumulated at this same discount rate). The "internal," or "implicit," rate of return paid by social security is that discount rate which equates these two.

Table 13 shows the rates of return paid by social security to single male workers at different income levels. The workers are assumed to enter the labor market at age twenty, retire at age sixty-five, and draw a retirement pension for ten years.[7] Their incomes are assumed to grow at a real rate of both 1.5 and 2.0 percent.

Rates of Return Examined

Basic Assumptions. The rates of return shown in table 13 are based on several assumptions about tax rates: (1) Roughly 75 percent of the 18.5 percent payroll tax rate as of April 1978 (13.79 percent) was attributed to retirement pensions. (2) As the system grows to maturity, payroll tax rates are expected to rise by 1.5–2.0 percentage points,[8] reaching 20.5 percent of taxable income in twenty years. Of this amount, 15.79 percent of taxable income (roughly 77 percent of the tax) has been attributed to retirement pensions. (3) In all cases, the worker is assumed to bear the full burden of the payroll tax. The flat-rate pension is assumed to be wage indexed, since this provision was in force at the time when most companies with occupational pension plans decided to contract out.

[7] The most recent actuarial tables show that in England and Wales, a male who is 20 years of age can expect to live another 51.2 years. These tables are revised every decade or so, however, and the revised tables usually show an increase in life expectancy at every age level. For this reason, a 20-year-old's actual life expectancy is probably closer to 55 years than 51.2 years. See Government Statistical Service, *Abstract of Statistics, 1976* (London: HMSO, 1976), table 34.

[8] See "Government Launches New Pension Scheme," press release (London: Department of Health and Social Security, February 27, 1975), p. A12.

TABLE 13

ESTIMATES OF RATES OF RETURN FOR SINGLE MALE WORKERS FULLY
PARTICIPATING IN NEW PENSION SYSTEM, WITH DIFFERENT ASSUMED
RATES OF GROWTH OF REAL WAGES
(percent)

Income Level per Week (£)	1.5 Percent Growth		2.0 Percent Growth	
	Initial rate of return[a]	Rate of return at maturity[b]	Initial rate of return[a]	Rate of return at maturity[b]
120	−0.4	−0.7	−0.2	−0.5
110	−0.3	−0.6	−0.1	−0.4
100	−0.3	−0.5	−0.1	−0.4
90	−0.2	−0.5	0	−0.3
80	−0.1	−0.4	0.1	−0.2
70	0	−0.3	0.3	0
60	0.2	−0.2	0.5	0.2
50	0.5	0.1	0.8	0.4
40	0.9	0.5	1.3	0.8
30	1.6	1.1	2.0	1.6
20	2.8	2.3	3.3	2.8

NOTE: Figures are based on April 1978 values. Worker enters the labor market at age twenty at the appropriate income level and retires, at age sixty-five, for ten more years. Income grows at a rate equal to the rate of growth of average wages.
[a] Payroll tax allocation: 13.79 percent of taxable income.
[b] Payroll tax allocation: 15.79 percent of taxable income.
SOURCE: Author.

Returns for Young Workers from Full Participation. The most re-markable feature of table 13 is the very low rate of return paid to young workers with average incomes. An average worker ought theoretically to receive a real rate of return equal to the real rate of growth of average wages. Before maturity, a pay-as-you-go system should be able to pay a real rate of return above the real rate of growth of average wages. Several studies of the social security system in the United States have concluded that if real wages in the United States grew at an annual rate of 1.75 percent, social security in the United States would pay young workers a real rate of return equal to about 1.5 percent.[9]

[9] See Robert Kaplan, "A Comparison of Rates of Return to Social Security Retirees under Wage and Price Indexing," and Martin Feldstein and Anthony Pellechio, "Social Security Wealth: The Impact of Alternative Inflation Adjustments," in Colin D. Campbell, ed., *Financing Social Security* (Washington, D.C.: American Enterprise Institute, 1979), pp. 91–117.

TABLE 14

RATE OF RETURN FOR A ONE-WORKER COUPLE, WITH A RATE OF
GROWTH OF REAL WAGES OF 1.5 PERCENT
(percent)

Income Level per Week (£)	Interim Pension Scheme[a]	Full Participation, New Pension System		Contracted Out, New Pension System	
		Initial rate of return[b]	Rate of return at maturity[c]	Initial rate of return[d]	Rate of return at maturity[e]
120	0.7	0.1	−0.5	−4.4	−5.2
110	0.9	0.3	−0.3	−3.9	−4.8
100	1.1	0.5	−0.1	−3.4	−4.2
90	1.3	0.7	0.1	−2.9	−3.7
80	1.5	1.0	0.4	−2.3	−3.1
70	1.8	1.3	0.7	−1.6	−2.4
60	2.2	1.6	1.1	−0.8	−1.7
50	2.6	2.1	1.5	0.1	−0.8
40	3.1	2.6	2.1	1.1	0.2
30	3.8	3.3	2.9	2.5	1.5
20	4.9	4.4	3.9	4.7	3.4

NOTE: These figures are based on April 1978 values. Husband enters the labor market at age twenty at the appropriate income level and retires at age sixty-five. Income grows at a rate equal to the rate of growth of average wages. Both spouses live ten years beyond the retirement age.
[a] Payroll tax allocation = 12 percent of taxable earnings.
[b] Payroll tax allocation = 13.79 percent of taxable earnings.
[c] Payroll tax allocation = 15.79 percent of taxable earnings.
[d] Payroll tax allocation = 13.79 percent of earnings up to the lower earnings limit and 6.79 percent of earnings between the earnings limits (abatement rate = 7 percent).
[e] Payroll tax allocation = 15.79 percent of earnings up to the lower earnings limit and 10.79 percent of earnings between the earnings limits (abatement rate = 5 percent).
SOURCE: Author.

Table 13 shows that workers in Britain will receive a much lower rate of return than that estimated for the United States. If wages grow at 1.5 percent per year, a British worker earning the average wage of eighty pounds per week will realize a negative rate of return, assuming no increase in tax rates. If wages grow at 2 percent per year, he will receive a rate of return of only 0.1 percent at initial tax rates.

Tables 14 and 15 show that married couples fare much better than the single worker. This is because the rate of return for a couple is calculated on the assumption that the dependent spouse pays no

TABLE 15

RATE OF RETURN FOR A ONE-WORKER COUPLE, WITH A RATE OF GROWTH OF REAL WAGES OF 2 PERCENT
(percent)

Income Level per Week (£)	Interim Pension Scheme[a]	Full Participation, New Pension System		Contracted Out, New Pension System	
		Initial rate of return[b]	Rate of return at maturity[c]	Initial rate of return[d]	Rate of return at maturity[e]
120	1.2	0.6	0	−3.9	−4.8
110	1.4	0.8	0.2	−3.4	−4.3
100	1.5	1.0	0.4	−2.9	−3.8
90	1.8	1.2	0.6	−2.4	−3.2
80	2.0	1.5	0.9	−1.7	−2.6
70	2.3	1.8	1.2	−1.1	−1.9
60	2.7	2.1	1.6	0	−1.2
50	3.1	2.6	2.1	0.5	−0.3
40	3.6	3.1	2.6	1.6	0.7
30	4.3	3.9	3.4	3.0	2.0
20	5.4	4.9	4.5	5.2	3.9

NOTE: These figures are based on April 1978 values. Husband enters the labor market at age twenty at the appropriate income level and retires at age sixty-five. Income grows at a rate equal to the rate of growth of average wages. Both spouses live ten years beyond the retirement age.
[a] Payroll tax allocation = 12 percent of taxable earnings.
[b] Payroll tax allocation = 13.79 percent of taxable earnings.
[c] Payroll tax allocation = 15.79 percent of taxable earnings.
[d] Payroll tax allocation = 13.79 percent of earnings up to the lower earnings limit and 6.79 percent of earnings between the earnings limits (abatement rate = 7 percent).
[e] Payroll tax allocation = 15.79 percent of earnings up to the lower earnings limit and 10.79 percent of earnings between the earnings limits (abatement rate = 5 percent).
SOURCE: Author.

taxes and will be able to draw a dependent's pension equal to about 60 percent of the husband's basic pension.

The rates of return estimated for couples overstate the return they will receive because only a small minority of British women will go through life without participating in the labor market. Among members of the generation entering the labor market today, most women will probably have earned pensions in their own right.

Even so, the rates calculated for couples are not particularly high. At initial tax rates, a couple earning a weekly income of eighty pounds receives a rate of return between 1 and 1.5 percent. Later, when the scheme reaches maturity and tax rates are raised, a couple with the average income will receive a rate of return of less than 1 percent.

Returns for Workers Contracted Out. Tables 14 and 15 show rates of return for couples contracted out. These rates of return are also fairly low. At initial tax rates, the contracted-out couple earning eighty pounds per week is promised a negative rate of return. At maturity, the system promises this contracted-out couple a return of −1.9 percent or less.

Explanations of the Relatively Low Rates of Return. Why are the rates of return promised by the new pension system lower than one would expect? One explanation is that these calculations contain a downward bias. Another explanation is that the low rates of return reflect the effects of the new system of contracting out.

Earnings Profiles. One source of bias is that the earnings profile of workers may be different from the hypothetical profile used in making the calculations. The calculations in tables 13, 14, and 15 assume that a worker enters the labor market at a certain wage level and enjoys wage increases in line with the general increase in average wages. This is a common assumption in the absence of better information about the actual earnings histories of workers and their families.[10] Evidence compiled by a recent report of the Consultant Panel on Social Security indicates, however, that (wage-indexed) earnings for a typical worker in the United States will tend to rise continuously until the worker reaches age fifty and will thereafter decline.[11] A typical worker, then, will receive a real income at age twenty that is about 27 percent of his real wage at age fifty. At retirement, his real income will be about 92 percent of real income at age fifty.

If British workers have similar wage patterns, a worker whose average lifetime income is £80 per week, for example, will be earning about £22 per week at age twenty and about £96 per week at age fifty (rather than £80 per week each week throughout his working career). Similarly, a worker whose average lifetime income is about £100 per week will tend to enter the labor market at a wage of about

---

[10] See, for example, John Brittain, *The Payroll Tax for Social Security* (Washington, D.C.: Brookings Institution, 1972), ch. 6.

[11] See U.S. Congress, Congressional Research Service, Consultant Panel on Social Security, *Reports Prepared for the Use of the Committee on Finance and the Committee on Ways and Means of the U.S. House of Representatives*, 94th Cong., 2d sess., August 1976, esp. pp. 89–90.

£27 per week and will earn about £120 per week by the time he reaches fifty.

The possible variations in earnings over a worker's lifetime are important because they affect the value of social security taxes paid. Because of the time value of money, a worker is better off if he can defer more of his taxes from earlier years to later years. Accordingly, recognition of the actual pattern of tax collection would probably raise the estimated rates of return for most workers.

Another reason why possible variations in earnings are important relates to the role of the maximum earnings limit. A British worker whose average income was equal to the maximum earnings limit and whose earnings history matched the profile of a typical worker in the United States would spend most of his working career earning an income above the maximum earnings limit and in most years would not pay social security taxes on all of his income.

On the basis of a typical earnings profile, a worker whose average income was £120 per week would be earning £144 per week at age fifty. Rather than pay 16 percent of his income in taxes at age fifty he would pay only 13 percent. The pattern of lifetime earnings for this worker would result in lower tax rates and a better deal from social security than for a worker who earned £120 per week every week.

Table 16 illustrates how the maximum earnings limit benefits workers at selected income levels. Workers whose average income exceeds £100 per week will benefit from the earnings limit. Moreover, the higher the average income, the greater the benefit. A worker averaging £105 per week can expect to earn more than the earnings limit in about twenty working years. A worker averaging £120 per week can expect to earn more than the earnings limit in more than thirty working years.

Another reason why rates of return in Britain are so low is that contracting out has probably lowered them. Suppose, for example, that 35 percent of the labor force were able to opt out of the social security system completely. This would mean that the burden of financing the benefits of those who have already retired would fall on the remaining 65 percent of the labor force. Those workers who remained in the system would have to pay higher tax rates in relation to their promised benefits, and their rates of return would be lower. Initially, the number of beneficiaries would not be reduced by contracting out, even though eventually it would be, when persons who have contracted out retire.

Allowing workers to opt out of the system initially reduces the

64

TABLE 16

Number of Years in Which Earnings Exceed Maximum Earnings Limit

Average Income per Week (£)	Income per Week at Age 50 (£)	Years above Limit
100	120	0
105	126	20
110	131	25
115	138	30
120	144	30

NOTE: The maximum earnings limit is £120 per week. The figures above are based on a typical lifetime profile of wage-indexed earnings in U.S. labor markets. See Congressional Research Service, Consultant Panel on Social Security, *Reports Prepared for the Use of the Committee on Finance of the U.S. Senate and the Committee on Ways and Means of the U.S. House of Representatives*, 94th Cong., 2d sess. (Washington, D.C.: CRS, August 1976), figure 1 and table 2.
SOURCE: Author.

ratio of taxpayers to beneficiaries and tends to leave the remaining taxpayers with a less favorable deal than they had before. Of course, contracting out under the British system is not complete. Workers are only able to opt out of the earnings-related tier. Nonetheless, partial opting out has the same kind of effect that would be produced by complete opting out. Tables 13, 14, and 15 illustrate that contracting out tends, on the average, to lower the estimated rates of return that young British workers who enter the labor force in 1979 earn on their social security taxes.

The low rates of return do not by themselves explain the inducement to contract out. As shown in tables 14 and 15, at every weekly income level above twenty pounds, contracted-out workers receive a rate of return on social security taxes no larger than the rate of return paid to fully participating workers. This is true both at initial tax rates and when the system reaches maturity.

Social Security Wealth

Although it would appear that there is little advantage to contracting out, the appearance is quite deceptive. The burden of participation in social security depends not only on the rate of return received on social security taxes but also on what alternative opportunities are available in the private capital market. For example, if social security pays a worker a 5 percent real rate of return, whereas his payroll tax dollars could have earned a 3 percent real rate of return if invested elsewhere, the worker receives a net benefit as a result of participation in social security. The present value of this net benefit may be called the worker's *net social security wealth*. On the other hand, if social security promises a worker a 1 percent real rate of return, whereas his payroll tax dollar could have earned a 3 percent rate of return if invested elsewhere, the worker bears a net burden. In this case, the worker's net social security wealth would be negative.

To calculate the value of net social security wealth for individuals entering the British labor market today, we adopted the same assumptions Feldstein and Pellechio used for the United States. They assume that real wages grow at 1.75 percent per year and that the real rate of interest paid by the private capital market is 3 percent.[12]

Given the historical rates of return paid by common stocks in both the United States and Great Britain, the 3 percent assumption is conservative. Nonetheless, it is higher than the rates of return promised to most young workers, as calculated in tables 13, 14, and 15. As a consequence, most workers entering the British labor market today have negative net social security wealth. The magnitude of the burden is quite large for most of them.

Table 17 shows the net values of social security wealth for a single worker at different income levels on the basis of initial tax rates. A worker earning the minimum earnings limit of £17.50 per week (£910 a year) has positive net social security wealth amounting to nearly £600. He receives a rate of return on the payroll taxes he pays that is slightly greater than 3 percent. As a result, the value of his social security pension is worth nearly £600 more than investing the same amount at the assumed rate of return in private markets of 3 percent. At only slightly higher income levels, however, social security wealth becomes negative. For example, the £80-per-week worker (£4,160 a year) fully participating in the new system faces a net burden of about £13,773. The £120-per-week worker (£6,240 a year) who is fully participating faces a net burden of £22,960.

Once the new pension system reaches maturity, tax rates are expected to be higher than they are currently. Table 18 shows the value of net social security wealth for young workers based on a 2 percentage point increase in payroll tax rates. The burden on the £80-per-week worker (£4,160 a year) rises by £2,857—from £13,793 to about £16,630.

[12] See Feldstein and Pellechio, "Social Security Wealth," pp. 91–117.

TABLE 17

Net Social Security Wealth, at Initial Tax Rates, for Single
Male Workers Participating Fully and Contracted Out
(pounds)

Annual Income	Full Participation	Contracted Out
910	597	597
1,040	22	29
1,560	− 2,276	− 922
2,080	− 4,574	− 2,137
2,600	− 6,873	− 3,352
3,120	− 9,171	− 4,567
3,640	− 11,469	− 5,782
4,160	− 13,773	− 6,997
4,680	− 16,066	− 8,212
5,200	− 18,364	− 9,427
5,720	− 20,662	− 10,642
6,240	− 22,960	− 11,857

NOTE: The figures describe the new pension system at initial tax rates. Worker enters the labor market at age twenty at the appropriate income level and retires at age sixty-five for ten more years. Real rate of growth of wages = 1.75 percent. Real rate of interest = 3 percent. Net social security wealth at most income levels is negative because the present value of tax payments exceeds the present value of benefit payments.
SOURCE: Author.

Workers Contrasted

Tables 17 and 18 show that at initial tax rates the net burden on fully participating workers is about twice the size of the net burden on contracted-out workers. When the system reaches maturity, the gap between the two groups of workers narrows considerably, especially if the abatement rate falls from 7 to 5 percent. Nonetheless, even at maturity, a worker will be better off if he can manage to contract out. The reason why contracting out is advantageous, even though the contracted-out worker may receive a similar rate of return on the taxes he paid in as a fully participating worker, is that contracting out enables him to invest a larger percentage of his savings for retirement at a higher rate of return than he gets from social security.

If social security is viewed in terms of its effect on personal wealth, contracted-out employees, along with other employees, have

TABLE 18

Net Social Security Wealth, at Maturity, for Single Male Workers Participating Fully and Contracted Out
(pounds)

Annual Income	Full Participation	Contracted Out	
		5% Abatement	7% Abatement
910	−30	−30	−36
1,040	−694	−512	−423
1,560	−3,350	−2,443	−1,996
2,080	−6,006	−4,374	−3,568
2,600	−8,662	−6,304	−5,141
3,120	−11,318	−8,235	−6,714
3,640	−13,974	−10,166	−8,287
4,160	−16,630	−12,065	−9,860
4,680	−19,286	−14,027	−11,433
5,200	−21,942	−15,958	−13,006
5,720	−24,599	−17,889	−14,578
6,240	−27,099	−19,819	−16,151

NOTE: The figures describe the new pension system at maturity. Worker enters the labor market at age twenty at the appropriate income level and retires at age sixty-five for ten more years. Real rate of growth of average wages = 1.75 percent. Real rate of interest = 3 percent. Net social security wealth at most income levels is negative because the present value of tax payments exceeds the present value of benefit payments.
SOURCE: Author.

less personal wealth than they would otherwise have had. What is true of this generation of workers will also be true of each succeeding generation. This does not necessarily mean that social security is an undesirable institution. Virtually all of the taxes taken from workers are given to nonworkers. These transfers, by themselves, do not make society as a whole worse off.[13] A worker's negative net social security wealth can be viewed as the price he has to pay for participating in a pay-as-you-go pension system. Such a system may provide other, nonfinancial benefits to the worker—such as the knowledge that retirees are receiving a minimum income without the use of a means test.

[13] The social costs of social security are the lower output levels that result if labor market participation is discouraged by the payroll tax and the lower growth rate for society that results if social security lowers the overall level of saving and therefore investment.

5

The Effects of Contracting Out

The policy of contracting out is important in several ways. For one thing, the government is relieved of the responsibility of providing second-tier pensions for a large number of British workers. Moreover, because a group can be contracted out only if its private pension plan provides benefits at least as good as those promised by the government, most workers contracting out will not require government assistance. Workers participating in private pension plans will tend to have above average incomes.

Contracting out is also important because of the expected effects on investment and economic growth. British social security, like most social security programs throughout the world, is run as a pay-as-you-go system. This means that it is essentially an income transfer program—money taken from the paychecks of those who are working is promptly transferred to those who are not working. It also means that most of the money transferred is ultimately allocated to consumption rather than to investment spending.

Private pension funds, by contrast, provide an important source of funds for private investment. Contributions to a private pension are invested during a worker's years of employment. Consumption does not occur until the worker retires and begins drawing his pension.

Although there is some dispute about the magnitude of these effects, on balance the evidence suggests that social security contributions are a substitute for private savings (and therefore investment).[1] This means that a great many social security tax dollars would have been invested in the absence of the social security payroll tax. As a result, allowing workers to substitute private pensions for na-

[1] The first important study, made by Martin Feldstein, estimated that the social security system in the United States reduced private savings by 38 percent in 1971. See Martin Feldstein, "Social Security, Induced Retirement and Aggregate Capital Accumulation," *Journal of Political Economy*, vol. 82 (September/October 1974), pp. 905–26. For a recent review of the literature that is critical of the "savings effect," see Louis Esposita, "Effect of Social Security on Saving: Review of Studies Using Time-Series Data," *Social Security Bulletin*, May 1978, pp. 9–17.

tional insurance should result in more investment than would otherwise occur.

At the present time it is not known precisely how many British workers are covered by contracted-out pension plans, although estimates range from 10.5 to 11 million, about 45 percent of the labor force. The ages, earnings, and length of service of these workers are also unknown. As a result, there has been no attempt to estimate what impact contracting out has had on overall investment in Britain.

There is some indirect evidence that contracting out has had an important effect, however. From 1974 to 1979, net investment in Britain fell from 13 percent to 8 percent of national income. Over the same period of time, the net amount of funds made available for investment by occupational pension schemes climbed from 5.5 percent to 6.6 percent of national income.[2] Private pension funds therefore appear to be furnishing a substantial and increasing share of investment funds in Britain. Since the act creating the new national pension system was passed in 1975, a reasonable inference is that the policy of contracting out is partly responsible for the development.

Finally, the policy of contracting out allows workers a great deal of flexibility and freedom of choice in shaping their own pension plans. Under a contracting-out plan, the workers themselves can negotiate for a plan which includes a retirement age, death-in-service benefits, and other pension characteristics that are tailored to their needs and preferences. This flexibility is greatly reduced to the degree that workers are forced to participate in a uniform national pension plan.

The British system of contracting out, therefore, has three attractive features: (1) lower long-run funding commitments for the social security system, (2) greater incentives for private saving and investment, and (3) more flexibility in the shaping of pension plans. These features are important and well worth the scrutiny of policy makers in the United States.

The mechanics of the British system of contracting out, however, are not necessarily ideal. All British workers who contract out of the second tier of the national pension plan do so on the same terms; that is, each receives the same reduction in payroll taxes, regardless of age, sex, or occupation. These terms are especially favorable to young workers, especially young male workers. They are unfavorable to older workers, especially older female workers.

[2] Central Statistical Office, *National Income and Expenditure* (London: HMSO, 1980), pp. 3, 31.

70

This feature of the British system of contracting out has three undesirable consequences. First, it necessarily means that the choice to contract out must be a group decision (nominally placed with the employer) rather than an individual decision. Were the option to contract out left to individual workers, the system would face all of the problems inherent in a totally voluntary social security system.

Second, this feature of the British system raises important questions of equity. Young workers who have managed to contract out have experienced a substantial increase in wealth relative to young workers who are fully participating. The magnitude of this wealth transfer may be partially ameliorated through compensating wage variations in the labor market. Nonetheless, the system of contracting out initially generates substantial, and somewhat arbitrary, transfers of wealth among British workers.

Third, the initial payroll tax abatement for contracted-out employees, along with the planned reduction in that abatement, will tend to create and perpetuate a condition under which half of all British workers are contracted out, while the other half fully participate. The initial terms for contracting out were quite attractive to firms that already had fully developed occupational pension schemes. As time passes, however, it will become more and more difficult for a new private pension plan to meet the terms for contracting out.

These undesirable consequences could be avoided by allowing the terms for contracting out to vary from worker to worker. For example, there is no reason why the terms for contracting out could not be structured so that young contracted-out workers get small tax reductions while older contracted-out workers get larger reductions. Workers nearing the retirement age might even be given a negative tax (a subsidy) in return for contracting out.

By allowing the tax incentive for contracting out to vary with the worker's age, and perhaps with sex and occupation as well, a workable system of contracting out could be constructed in which the option to contract out was left to the individual worker. Such a system could achieve greater flexibility and equity than the British system. It could also be designed so that new private pension plans are encouraged rather than discouraged as the system develops.

Britain, however, has had one advantage that the United States is not likely to have in terms of the politics of social security. During the start-up stage of a social security system, workers generally receive a high real rate of return on their "investment" in social security—a fact that tends to make the system politically popular. During the mature stage of a social security system, the rate of return will be very modest. During the winding-down stage—as represented by a system of contracting out—rates of return will be lower than in a mature stage. In fact, during a winding down stage, real rates of return are likely to be negative—a fact that may tend to make the process of winding down politically unpopular.

Winding down a social security system is painful because it generally means that workers must pay taxes to finance promised benefits for the current generation of retirees and at the same time accept lower promised retirement benefits for themselves.

The British were in the favorable position of being able to combine a start-up stage with a winding-down stage. The second tier, earnings-related pension plan, which began in 1978, will mature over a period of twenty years. Fully participating workers who now face higher social security taxes are also promised higher retirement benefits. Moreover, those workers who retire during the twenty-year start-up phase of this plan can generally expect to receive a high real rate of return.

Were the United States to adopt a system of contracting out, it would probably be a "pure" winding down of the social security system. In order to induce workers to contract out and agree to accept lower social security benefits, they would have to be given reductions in social security taxes. Yet in order to continue to finance retirement benefits for current retirees, taxes would have to be increased for fully participating workers.

This would mean that fully participating workers would face higher social security taxes and no increase in promised social security benefits. Undoubtedly there will be strong political pressures to resist such a change.